ESSAYS ON THE POLITICIANS OF WALES THROUGH THE AGES

Jonathan Morgan

Print ISBN 978-0-9928690-0-7

Published by

Llyfrau Cambria Books, Wales, United Kingdom.

Cambria Books is the imprint of

Cambria Publishing Ltd.

Discover our other books at: www.cambriabooks.co.uk

This book is dedicated to Lord Paul Murphy, Lord Dafydd Wigley, Sir Paul Silk and former MP Roger Williams.

We thank the following for their financial assistance:

Colonel Tim Van Rees, Chris Thomas MA and the Old Breconians Charitable Trust.

Thank you to Frances Chaffey for her secretarial skills.

Illustrations by Robert Macdonald RWSW (President), MA (RCA), Diop.LCSAD.

Jonathan Morgan

Jonathan Morgan was born in Brecon, Wales. He was educated at Christ College Brecon and it was obvious to him that he came from one of Wales' great sporting families. After gaining a scholarship to RMA Sandhurst, he spent a number of years as an officer in the Royal Regiment of Wales. During this time, he studied British Government and Politics under Paul Murphy (who later became Lord Murphy); he also studied International Politics at Aberystwyth University.

Jonathan was invalided out of the army with PTSD or related illness. He has since written five books relating to Wales, having taught Modern Welsh Identity as one of his courses at Cardiff Metropolitan University.

Robert Macdonald

The illustrator Robert Macdonald went as a mature student to study painting at the Royal College of Art in 1976. He was 41 years old and had had an earlier career as a journalist in Fleet St. While writing on politics and foreign affairs he met a number of the contemporary politicians featured in this book.

For four years in the early 1970s he worked for the government news agency in the News Department of the Foreign Office, becoming chief diplomatic correspondent for the Central Office of Information and travelling widely with the then Foreign Minister James Callaghan.

Among many other journeys, he flew in 1975 to Uganda where Callaghan hoped to confront the dictator Idi Amin who was threatening to execute an imprisoned British lecturer on a charge of treason. They rescued the prisoner and returned safely to Britain. He draws on this episode lightly in his illustration of Callaghan, a man he admired and got to know 'quite well'.

More recently Kirsty Williams kindly performed the opening of one of his art exhibitions held near Brecon in Crickhowell.

FOREWORD

Sir Paul Silk

There is a tradition of biographical storytelling in historiography that goes back through Lytton Strachey, John Aubrey and Gaius Suetonius to Plutarch. Jonathan Morgan's new book is in that tradition.

He has described a set of politicians who have had a very wide range of impacts on history and who date from the sixteenth century to today. The definition of "politician" used is pretty wide – Amy Dillwyn and Raymond Williams could be regarded as political actors, but they would not normally be described as politicians. The leitmotif for the author (a passionate Welshman, though clearly no nationalist) is Wales, and Jonathan's subjects are united by having some connection to Wales (though in several cases, that connection is pretty tenuous: Richard Nixon, for example).

There is a particular, and understandable, bias towards Breconshire and to those who might be seen to hold views amenable to the author, or with whom he can empathise whether through shared faith or military experience.

Throughout we are given interesting details of the subjects' lives, sometimes at some length, occasionally in a pithy sentence or two; and we can read Jonathan's views of their contribution to history – views that are sometimes idiosyncratic, often unduly charitable, but always interesting because we hear the author speaking in his inimitable and endearing voice.

The volume is much enhanced by expert guest essays from Graham Lippiatt, Chris Thomas, James Gibson-Watt, Nick Thomas-Symonds and Robin Lewis.

It is a rollicking read.

CONTENTS

INTRODUCTION 1

THE 16TH CENTURY 4

   THE CECILS AND QUEEN ELIZABETH I 4

   DR JOHN DEE 7

THE 17TH CENTURY 9

   OLIVER CROMWELL formerly WILLIAMS 9

TWO DIFFERENT MPS IN THE 19TH CENTURY 13

   HENRY RICHARD 1812 – 1888 14

   WILLIAM EWART GLADSTONE 15

   THOMAS EDWARD ELLIS 1859 -1899 17

THE WELSH IN AMERICA 19

   JOHN ADAMS 1797-1801, JOHN QUINCY ADAMS 1825-
1829 20

   THOMAS JEFFERSON 20

   JAMES MONROE 1817-1825 22

   WILLIAM HARRISON 1841 22

   ABRAHAM LINCOLN 22

   JEFFERSON DAVIES 22

   JAMES A GARFIELD 23

   RICHARD NIXON 1969-71 23

   HILARY CLINTON 24

THE SUFFRAGETTES 25

   MARGARET HAIG THOMAS (LADY RHONDDA) 25

   AMY DILLWYN 26

ROSEMARY CRAWSHAY 26

POLITICAL GIANTS OF THE 20TH CENTURY 28

JAMES KEIR HARDIE..28

DAVID LLOYD GEORGE 30

GWILYM AND MEGAN LLOYD GEORGE......................38

GWENLLIAN MORGAN 43

THE GALLANT MEMBERS 45

MAJOR GENERAL IVOR PHILIPPS.......................45

LORD PETER THOMAS QC 54

DAVID GIBSON- WATT MC PC 55

ENOCH POWELL..59

LORD CHALFONT..61

NYE BEVAN AND JENNIE LEE 63

THE CONSERVATIVES in the 20th CENTURY....................69

DAVID VIVIAN PENROSE LEWIS 69

GEOFFREY HOWE..71

MICHAEL HESELTINE 72

MICHAEL HOWARD 75

TRISTAN GAREL-JONES......................................77

WILLIAM HAGUE 77

NICHOLAS EDWARDS, LORD CRICKHOWELL............78

SIR ROBERT BUCKLAND QC 79

RAYMOND WILLIAMS, ...81

THE LABOUR PARTY IN THE 20TH CENTURY 86

STEPHEN OWEN DAVIES 1886 – 1972..............86

JAMES GRIFFITHS 87

MICHAEL FOOT..88

JAMES CALLAGHAN 90

TUDOR ELWYN WATKINS, ... 91

LORD CLEDWYN 92

LORD ELWYN JONES 94

GEORGE THOMAS 95

PAUL MURPHY 97

THE KINNOCKS 98

BARON MORRIS OF ABERAVON 101

LEO ABSE 101

ANN CLWYD 102

LORD ELYSTAN MORGAN 104

MERLYN REES 105

THE MOVE TO THE ASSEMBLY 107

RON DAVIES.. 107

RHODRI MORGAN 108

THE LIBERALS AND LIBERAL DEMOCRATS 114

THE DAVIESES OF LLANDINAM 114

EMLYN HOOSON... 117

LORD GERAINT HOWELLS 119

SIR SIMON HUGHES.. 120

THE LIBERALS OF BRECON & RADNOR 122

RICHARD LIVSEY 122

ROGER WILLIAMS MP 123

KIRSTY WILLIAMS.. 125

PLAID CYMRU OVER THE YEARS............................ 127

SAUNDERS LEWIS 127

GWYNFOR EVANS.. 132

DAFYDD WIGLEY 133

DAFYDD ELIS-THOMAS 134

ADAM PRICE 135

THE SOCIAL DEMOCRATIC PARTY 136

LORD DAVID OWEN 136

ROY JENKINS 137

CONCLUSION 140

INTRODUCTION

I am a disabled war veteran who suffered from PTSD, partly as a result of a terrible tour of Northern Ireland in 1972. I also felt beleaguered in the Royal Regiment of Wales in a culture which seemed to treat the Welsh as colonial troops to be commanded by English public schoolboys. My great uncle Dr Teddy Morgan captained Wales and the British Lions at rugby, and my Uncle Guy captained Wales and Cambridge also at rugby. I was therefore ensconced in the Welsh sporting tradition.

There seemed to be an idea in the Regiment in the 1970s that Welsh officers were 2nd class citizens despite the fact thousands of them had died for their country in the 2 Great Wars. I, certainly, had a bit of an inferiority complex, which was played upon by rivals. Having studied International Politics at Aberystwyth University, I came back to Wales after my breakdown and being invalided out of the army I started to do research to see if the Welsh were really, 'A bunch of losers'. I soon realised that the last time a Welsh army had taken on an English army was at Bosworth in 1485 and the Welsh had won. I then went on to research a book on Welsh Entrepreneurs through the ages and discovered some of the biggest banking families were Welsh including JP Morgan, Lloyds and the Bevans of Barclays. In face of the aggression of the English in the City we could well hold our own. I went on to write a second book at the anniversary of the First World War on the Welsh war poets through the ages, and some of these include Wilfred Owen, Edward Thomas and David Jones.

I then returned to my own profession and wrote a book on the Welsh warrior through the ages, showing the Welsh had achieved the heights of bravery and high command throughout history. Now, I have turned to another strong hand, the politicians of Wales through time, which shows that the Welsh have been an integral part of the power centre at Westminster and have played a huge part in the formation of the United Kingdom. For instance, many people didn't

know that Oliver Cromwell came from a Welsh family, others didn't
know that Gladstone had married a Welsh wife and lived in Wales,
and that two of the greatest achievers in Welsh history, Nye Bevan
and Lloyd George, were from the Principality.

Nye Bevan

There have been times, such as the Battle of the Tryweryn Valley
flooding where the Welsh MPs united against the drowning but were
outvoted by English MPs. Certainly, the 18th century was short of
influential Welsh MPs, but before that at the time of the great Welsh
Queen, Elizabeth I, the Welsh were very influential including the
powerful Cecil family from Pandy, outside Abergavenny.

When the Liberals were in the ascendency, there was a very
powerful Welsh block of MPs and a lot of support for more powers
for Wales. This culminated eventually in a proposal for a Welsh
Secretary of State and more recently for an Assembly.

The Welsh Conservatives have always had some influence and it is
interesting that the reason why Margaret Thatcher is not featured
greatly in the book is because she replied to the author saying she had
no Welsh ancestry. Although John Campbell her biographer says her

father came from a Welsh family. There is an insinuation that she might have been ashamed of her Welsh roots, especially after her battle with the miners, although it is interesting and paradoxical that the Welsh Guards carried her coffin at her funeral.

It must be remembered that Wales is England's oldest ally and have stood with them certainly very prominently in the 100 Years War against France in which the Welsh archers played a key role. The Black Prince at Crecy where there were 2,000 Welsh archers dressed his bowmen in the green and white colours of Wales. Henry Tudor carried the Red Dragon at Bosworth. The somewhat disparaging attitude of the English establishment towards the Welsh belies one that should be based on mutual respect.

The Welsh are recognised throughout the world, especially in the United States where at least eight Presidents were of Welsh stock, including two of the greats, Jefferson and Lincoln. The politicians of Wales have played a huge part in the fortunes of the United Kingdom, and this should never be forgotten.

With regard to Wales, there is a movement towards independence and certainly as Wales is about the same size as Lithuania, Latvia and Estonia and has the precious possession of the world's most important commodity, water, Wales could probably sustain itself. But certainly, at the moment, the majority of the people don't seem to want independence and, in a democracy, they hold the trump card.

This book shows that the Welsh 'punch well above their weight!'.

However, we have got to remember that for a long period of time, the Welsh had only twenty-eight MPs and it was only later, in the 20th century this increased to forty. And more recently the Boundary Commission proposes to reduce the number again.

So Welsh influence in the Commons will decline.

THE 16TH CENTURY

THE CECILS AND QUEEN ELIZABETH I

One historian said that if you went to any Welsh market town in Elizabethan times, you would see women in the market who looked like Elizabeth 1, auburn hair and sharp features. Her looks reflected many of the characteristics of a Welsh woman of that time. There is no doubt that Elizabeth had a penchant f or her Welsh subjects.

The Cecils statesman came from a family typical of the new governing classes which rose to power under the Tudors - canny, ambitious and energetic. Their grandfather David, the youngest son of a poor Welsh squire left his home, a small, grey manor house buried in the remote green hills of the Wales Hereford border to follow Henry Tudor and his campaign for the crown. When he became King, Henry rewarded David Cecil by making him a Yeoman of the Guard. This was the foundation of the family fortunes. David raised enough money to buy a property near Stamford in Northamptonshire, where he distinguished himself enough to become mayor and a Member of Parliament. David's son Richard further consolidated the family fortune and was made a groom to the Privy Chamber. William, his elder son born in 1520, showed himself unusually clever and hard working. After a short period as Court Page and some time at Grantham Grammar School, he went up at the age of 14 to St John's College, Cambridge.

From the first, he was attracted by political life and when he left Cambridge, he joined the Inns of Court to learn the laws of the land. He became learned in the classics and also philosophy and was a firm but moderate protestant. His fortunes continued to prosper; he married Mildred Cooke who was the daughter of Sir Anthony Cooke, governor to the young Prince Edward. Henry VIII took him into his service and when he died, and the Duke of Somerset was made Lord Protector he appointed William to act as his personal Master of

Requests. He navigated his way through the reigns of E~~~
Mary without putting a foot wrong. When Elizabeth c~
throne, she knew him well enough to appoint him as one of
councillors. He always believed in moderation, in order, in pe~
compromise. He also believed in balance between parties at hom~ ~d
between forms of religious enthusiasm. He did not think even the
Queen was above the law. They never really disagreed and she always
fell back on William Cecil's advice. He was firmly in favour of Mary,
Queen of Scots execution, although the Queen was very ambivalent
over it.

Lord Burleigh

In 1571 Elizabeth created him Lord Burghley and a year later,
Knight of the Garter and Lord Treasurer. His was a sober house with
a magnificent library full of books on astronomy and geography. He
read in bed in English, French, Italian, Greek and Latin. He was fairly
indifferent to music and poetry. His garden also became famous. It
was filled with rare plants of interest to botanists. He loved beauty

which was demonstrated in the planning of his terraces and fountains and avenues.

On his death bed he could look back at his numerous achievements. He never fell out with the Queen, although he found both her favourites, Leicester and Essex difficult to deal with. She relied on him to the end, and when he died, his son Robert took over as the leading councillor in the realm. When Robert died, he had made the Cecils one of the first families in England.

However, to go back to Queen Elizabeth and her coterie of Welsh families: Dr John Dee she often relied upon in her exploration of astronomy and theology. He had a huge library on the Thames near Henley and was often in her favour. Sir John Herbert, who spoke Welsh was the 2nd Secretary of State, Sir Thomas Parry was her accountant, and Blanche Parry who was related to the Earls of Pembroke and owned land in Breconshire was one of her ladies of the bedchamber and who also possibly taught Elizabeth some Welsh. Robert Cecil as previously mentioned, the 1st Earl of Salisbury, was also a statesman, capable and dedicated. He was courteous and modest and grave, although his private character was more suspect. A reckless gambler and suspected of many love affairs. He'd grown up very short, with a crooked back and an awkward way of walking. He hated war and thought it ruinous. When Burghley was still alive, Robert, his son became a sort of unofficial Secretary of State. He did not get on with Essex, but it was Essex who came a cropper, and not Cecil.

His father, just before he died, told him 'to tend in all thy actions in the state, to shun foreign wars and seditions, labour with thy Prince's honour, to reconcile her to all her enemies so far as they stand with honour and safety, and thirdly to make sure to secure a successor to the Queen'. He always had to cope with the Queen, but like his father, he did not govern all things with her. She remained the ultimate authority. Elizabeth had a power to inspire devotion. Robert Cecil loved her better than any. It was Robert who with his ability to negotiate shrewdly wrought the changeover to James I after Elizabeth's death. He was not really at home in James's court but continued to serve the new King loyally. Together with Queen Elizabeth, they represent the wisdom of the age. England was well governed, so long as they were in full power. England was transformed from a mediaeval to a modern nation. Both men were basically reconcilers who kept a delicate balance in the Kingdom in virtually all realms. They were relied upon to support one of our greatest Queens. What has been called one of England's greatest political families originated, like the Tudors, from Wales. It is interesting in recent times, that Lord Ned Cecil bought Old Gwernyfed House in Breconshire and lived there for a time.

They never lost their original identity in Wales.

DR JOHN DEE

We should not forget the controversial Dr John Dee.

Dr John Dee was a mathematician, astronomer, astrologer, teacher, occultist and alchemist.

He was the court astronomer and adviser to Queen Elizabeth I. His father was Roland Dee, of Welsh descent. His surname Dee reflects the Welsh 'du', (black) and his grandfather was Bedo Ddu of Nantygroes, Pilleth in Radnorshire. He claimed to descend from Rhodri the Great, King of Wales. He had a lot of contact with Elizabeth and was very keen on establishing the British Empire. He is said to have told the Queen that she was one of the 'old Brits' and therefore it should be called the British Empire.

In his 'Title Royal' of 1580 he invented a claim that Madoc ap Owain Gwynedd had discovered America intending thereby to boost England's claim to the New World over that of Spain's. He also asserted that Brutus of Britain and King Arthur as well as Madoc had conquered lands in the Americas so that their heir Elizabeth I had a prior claim there.

He was an intense Christian and believed that numbers were the basis of all things and the key to knowledge. His goal was to help bring forth a unified world religion through the healing of the breach of the healing of the Roman Catholic Churches. He was an extraordinary man, influential at our time in court and had Elizabeth's ear. He had a renowned library at Mortlake but it was vandalised when he was on the European continent and unfortunately he ended up poor and almost bankrupt.

THE 17TH CENTURY

OLIVER CROMWELL formerly WILLIAMS

Although Oliver Cromwell only visited Wales twice, once to suppress several thousand of its rebellious inhabitants, then once en route to Ireland, he was, by descent, a Welshman.

Oliver Cromwell

Much was made under the protectorate under a heraldic point of view, of Cromwell's descent from the Princes of Powys. Cromwell's forebears were a very typical minor Welsh gentry family; they were said to be a brewing family from Glamorgan, and his great great grandfather was Morgan Williams who emigrated to England.

9

Eventually a change of surname was made to Cromwell, partly to curry favour with the infamous maternal uncle Thomas Cromwell.

Henry VIII disapproved of the 'aps' which made those of Welsh descent hard to identify in English judicial procedure and insisted on family names of a more substantial kind. Oliver's grandfather Henry Cromwell had been dubbed Knight by Queen Elizabeth I in 1563. By the 1600s the family had moved to Huntingdonshire but did not forget their Welsh heritage. In the magnificent house at Hinchinbroke, a family seat of much splendour, the stained-glass windows did not fail to commemorate the family's Welsh origins. In fact, when he was Lord Protector, Oliver was said to sign papers 'Cromwell born Williams'. The family commissioned family trees reaching back to ancient Welsh Princes, and as mentioned, filled their windows with heraldic glass showing their Welsh connections.

In the English Civil War Cromwell became one of the Parliamentarians greatest commanders. He was particularly good at commanding cavalry, and time and again when he, having defeated the opposite Royalist wing of cavalry, brought his troops round in good order to attack the Royalist centre. Whereas Prince Rupert would engage in ferocious charges, often defeating the opposite wing but his troops did not have the discipline to prevent rout, rape and pillage which took their minds off the battle. Cromwell again was highly instrumental in forming the New Model Army and imposing on it professional discipline. After the defeat of the King, his aggressive foreign policy and support for trade were praised unreservedly. Carlyle in his letters and speeches on Oliver Cromwell established that Cromwell was not, in the normal sense of the words, either ambitious or a hypocrite. When he took over, the country was trembling on the brink of democracy; he prevented a new autocracy with the King claiming divine right. He was often exasperated by Parliament, and although on the Puritan wing, had a healthy respect for those of independent conscience.

In 1648 he became a major Welsh landowner, taking lands from the Royalist Earl of Worcester. These included large estates in Monmouthshire and virtually all of the Gower peninsular. There is some evidence that Cromwell used these lands to support likeminded friends and associates and to drive forward the Puritanisation of a country that many saw as mired in religious ignorance. A project that was particularly close to Cromwell's heart was a commission for the propagation of the gospel in Wales 1650-1653. This was a state sponsored body which supported radical Puritans in their efforts to convert the people of Wales to a more reformed brand of Protestantism. Here was a Welsh hero working against religious ignorance and apathy in an effort to raise the spiritual condition of the beloved benighted country. A pamphlet from hundreds of Cromwell's Welsh supporters in 1656 praised 'His most Christian and favourable understanding of us, the poor saints of Wales who are so much your joy'.

After the Revolution, the King was no longer able to hold a position of supreme power over Parliament. Cromwell played a leading part in bringing Charles I to the scaffold. He tried to be the mediator between Charles and the army, but inevitably came down on the side of the army. Surprisingly, because of his democratic attitude to his troops, he opposed demands for manhood suffrage. He was never quite sure if his main duty was to the people of England or to the people of God. He was far more tolerant than most men of his time and class. Only in his intolerance to the Irish Papists did Cromwell fail to rise above the standards of his age.

Outside the army, he was fêted by the Radicals. He owed his position to the army, which he could never, as a last resort, break from. Oliver's real tolerance did not extend to Papists. The massacres of Drogheda and Wexford, were laid at Cromwell's door. There were few mitigating circumstances. He followed the maxim of 'Trust in God and keep your powder dry'. He believed God intervened directly in history. His theory of government always aimed towards that which was ultimately established in 1688. He struggled for that settlement in his own time. The Puritan revolution under him failed, but there were economic, political and constitutional revolutions that took place. His tolerance extended to the Jews, but after the Restoration and his death, his corpse was solemnly exhumed from Westminster

Abbey. It was dragged through the streets of London from Holborn to Tyburn on open hurdles. The body was hung up in full gaze of the public, then taken down and the common hangman proceeded to hack off it's head. The headless trunk was consigned into a deep pit dug beneath the gallows of Tyburn and the head was taken down to Westminster and five days later stuck on a pole of oak where it mouldered in a state of decomposition until 1684. The story goes that it was blown down in a monster gale at the end of the reign of James II, falling at the feet of one of the sentinels. The skull was picked up by a man who hid it under his cloak, and it eventually passed into the hands of a dissolute and drunk actor called Samuel Russell and was later acquired by James Cox, proprietor of a museum. He in turn sold it to speculators who exhibited it at the time of the French Revolution. It eventually came into the hands of Canon Wilkinson, who left it to Cromwell's old College of Sidney Sussex. Cromwell's statue stands outside the Houses of Parliament in a very prominent position. He became a dictator but he lay the foundations of a future Parliamentary democracy. So, in a way, he is a Parliamentary hero.

He was the far-sighted politician whose bold revolution fatally undermined the power of the monarchy and set the country on the road to a modern constitution. The humble champion of individual liberties against oppression by the mighty; the advocate of toleration who readmitted Jews to England after more than 350 years of exile.

Paradoxically he never exercised his democracy in Ireland, where he is remembered for his cruelty and unforgiving religious discrimination. He was hated in Ireland for generations and remains so. It is a pity that a man with such democratic credentials should have let himself down in this way.

TWO DIFFERENT MPS IN THE 19TH CENTURY

Colonel Vaughan Watkins was first elected mayor of Brecon in January 1836. He was, for many years, a prominent member of the Common Council, a Worshipful Master of the first Board of Health, Justice of the Peace, High Sheriff (1836), and Lord Lieutenant from 1847 until 1865. He was also Liberal MP for the borough.

He rebuilt Penoyre House, which was said to have cost him £100,000, a huge sum of money in those days. However, heavy taxes, the outlay on building the mansion together with its upkeep all proved a great strain on the Colonel's resources. He was a man of great generosity to personal friends and to the locality in general. But the time came when he could no longer afford to live in the mansion he had built, and he was compelled to move from this palatial residence into the Old Bear Hotel in Ship Street, Brecon.

The last days of the Colonel were spent in comparative poverty; nevertheless, he retained to the end the respect and affection of the people of Brecon. And when he died, a very large gathering attended his funeral which was accompanied by much civil and military ceremonial seldom seen in the district before. He was interred in the family vault in Llandefaelog. He was a very substantial and good man, who fell on hard times.

In the same century as Vaughan Watkins was Charles Morgan, First Baron Tredegar.

He was first elected Member of Parliament for Brecon in 1812 and was re elected in 1830 and 1835. He served in the militia, becoming a commander and was appointed High Sheriff of Breconshire for 1850-51. He was Lord Lieutenant of the same county from 1866 until his death. He was a landowner and industrialist and though a diehard Conservative in his views who supported Wellington as Prime

Minister, he stood as a Whig.

These two MPs are examples of the genre at the time which really showed you had to have wealth to stand for that position.

HENRY RICHARD 1812 – 1888

He was born in Tregaron, Cardiganshire in 1812, and was a son of the Reverend Ebenezer Richard. He received his education in a school at Llangeitho and at Highbury Independent College London. He was the Minister of Marlborough Congregational Church London from 1835 until 1850 and for the rest of his life was prominent in his activities as an Apostle of Peace and Member for Wales.

He was appointed Secretary of the Peace Society in 1848 which was a very important time for conferences on peace which were held in such places as Brussels, Paris and Frankfurt. He was a close friend of Cobden and John Bright, and he edited the Peace Society's monthly magazine.

He was deeply interested in Wales still and was adamant in his protest against the Blue Books in 1847. He was a member of the Liberal Party and was elected Member of Parliament for Merthyr in 1868 and continued to be its member until his death. His main interests were the land question, religion and the state, education and peace. He protested against the Cardiganshire landowners who evicted their tenants from their farms because of their religious and political views. He was a member of the Departmental Committee which was appointed to consider the problem of higher education in Wales, and also of the Royal Commission on Education in England and Wales. He was always keen to support the cause of peace and also the idea of international arbitration. He was elected Chairman of the Congregational Union for England and Wales for the year 1877 and was the first layman to be chosen.

WILLIAM EWART GLADSTONE

Gladstone was born in Liverpool. He had no roots in Wales. He went to school at Eton and went to Oxford in 1828. He married into the Glynne family, a Welsh family, marrying Catherine Glynne. They lived in Hawarden which was a large, landed estate on the borders of Cheshire and North Wales. He lived for nearly 89 years, spending 63 years in the House of Commons, 27 of them in office and 12 as Prime Minister. He read over 20,000 books, he chopped down innumerable trees, he could walk vast distances either in Snowdonia or in the Scottish Highlands. He was a dedicated student of the works of Homer. In many ways, religion was more important to him than politics.

William Ewart Gladstone

He made many mistakes, failed in his last major objective of home rule for Ireland and left behind him a demoralised and squabbling Liberal Party. Gladstone had little specific sympathy with the Non-Conformist radicalism that emerged in Wales following the election of 1868. During the long campaign for the disestablishment of the Church in Wales, Gladstone showed a persistent resistance to commit himself to public action. When he finally retired from public life, there is no doubt that the political fortunes of Wales had been enormously advanced. The Reform Act of 1884 had liberated the rural vote and the mining proletariat in South Wales.

Throughout the period up to 1886, Gladstone gave many indications that the Church in Wales did call for separate treatment. He was keen to encourage a trend for native Welshmen to be Bishops in Wales. In the election of 1885, of the 34 Welsh members returned, 30 were Liberals and half of these Non-Conformists. Gladstone had conceded that it was impossible to place Wales with its clearly marked nationality and its difference from England with both race and language upon the same footing as an English town or district. He was instrumental in giving grants to the Universities of Bangor and Cardiff.

The election of 1886 saw the Liberal Party lose its majority in England and they became dependent on their strength in Scotland and Wales. As a symbol of Gladstone's growth of interest in Welsh questions was his friendship with Stuart Rendell who became Chairman of the new Welsh Independent Party.

When he visited South Wales in June 1887 he was greeted with enthusiasm and veneration by huge crowds of many thousands and he spoke warmly of the reality of Welsh nationality. For a long time, he always seemed ambivalent on Wales' disestablishment of the Welsh Church. After the election of 1892, 31 Liberals were returned in 34 Welsh seats. The Welsh Party of whom all except 9 were Welsh Non Conformists found themselves with the balance of power in their hands. He committed himself still further in his speech at Cwmllan near Snowdon in September 1892, where his warm references to Welsh nationality made a strong impression on Welsh opinion. The disastrous Liberal rout at the 1895 election led to 10 years of Unionist government and Welsh Political nationalism went into decline.

In Gladstone's later period came the most creative period of Welsh political descent. In one direction after another, in education, in the church, in land reform and in temperance matters, Welsh nationality was recognised. 'I affirm that Welsh nationality is as great a reality as English nationality', so he said towards the end of his life.

It is therefore possible to include Gladstone as a politician of Wales. His party held the preponderance of seats, and he was inclined to listen to Welsh Non-Conformity. He was for extending the vote, and for such fundamental principles as free trade. He was one of the great Prime Ministers, 4 times being in that job. He loved Hawarden and spent much time there. He had a Welsh wife and felt much closeness to Wales.

THOMAS EDWARD ELLIS 1859 -1899

Tom Ellis was the most prominent spokesman for the cause of Wales at the close of the 19th century.

He was born in Cefnddwysarn near Bala. He was the third of 8 children to a tenant farmer. He attended Bala Grammar School and his student years were at Aberystwyth and Oxford.

He was elected as Liberal MP for Merionethshire in 1886 and had huge enthusiasm for the cause of home rule for Wales. He wanted the control of the liquor trade, taxation, public appointments, and the means of national development in the hands of the Welsh. He became a leading figure in Cymru Fydd, a pressure group looking to Wales in the future.

He was however appointed Wales chief whip in 1894 and therefore did not seek to rock the Liberal boat in the 1890s. He was considered a really nice person and wasn't really up to the rough and tumble of Liberal politics in the post Gladstonian era.

His death in 1899 was untimely, and he was widely mourned as a huge advocate for the cause of Wales and his statue now stands prominently in Bala High Street.

A substantial Celtic Cross marks his grave in his home village cemetery.

THE WELSH IN AMERICA

Richard Price was a Welsh moral philosopher, non-conformist preacher and mathematician. He was also a political pamphleteer, active in radical republican and liberal causes such as the American Revolution. He spent most of his adult life as Minister of Newington Green Unitarian Church on the outskirts of London. He was also a Fellow of the Royal Society. He was born at Tynton, a farmhouse in the village of Llangeinor in Glamorgan. He was educated privately, then at Neath and Pentwyn. He studied under Vavasor Griffiths at Talgarth, Powys. He was part of the Bowood Circle, a group of liberal intellectuals around Lord Shelburne. He was a part of the group that Benjamin Franklin christened, 'The Club of Honest Whigs'. At home or in his church he was visited by Benjamin Franklin, Thomas Jefferson and Thomas Paine and other American politicians such as John Adams. The support Price gave to the Colonies on British North America in the American War of Independence made him famous.

In early 1776 he published, 'Observations on the Nature of Civil Liberty', 'The Principles of Government' and 'The Justice and Policy of the War with America'. 60,000 copies of this last pamphlet were sold within days and a cheap edition sold twice as many copies. He was presented with the Freedom of the City of London and it is said that his pamphlet had a part in the Americans determining to declare their independence. A second pamphlet was published on the war with America and the debts of Great Britain in the spring of 1777. Franklin was a close friend and in the winter of 1788 Price was invited by the Continental Congress to go to America and assist with the financial administration of the States.

In 1781 he alone, with George Washington, received the degree of 'Doctor of Laws' from Yale College. He preached to crowded congregations and when Lord Shelburne became Prime Minister in 1782 he was offered the post of his private secretary. The same year he was elected a foreign Honorary Member of the American

Academy of Arts and Sciences. In 1785 Price was elected an international member of the American Philosophical Society. Price also wrote, 'Observations on the Importance of the American Revolution and the Means of Rendering it a Benefit to the World'. It was well received by the Americans and it did suggest that the greatest problem facing Congress was its lack of central powers. He was also to write about the French Revolution and was fêted as a demographer and also as quite an expert on moral philosophy.

In terms of the past presidents of the United States with Welsh origin, there was John Adams, Thomas Jefferson, James Madison, John Quincy Adams, General WH Harrison, Abraham Lincoln and General Garfield.

JOHN ADAMS 1797-1801, JOHN QUINCY ADAMS 1825-1829

This father and son pair were the second and sixth presidents, John Adams played a key role in the peace negotiations with Great Britain and became the first president to live in the White House. His son was a leading opponent of slavery. Their ancestry has been traced back to Penybanc Farm in Llanboidy Carmarthenshire. According to author Phil Carradice the earliest reference to his family comes in 1422 when a distant ancestor

John Adams of Pembroke married the daughter of Penybanc Farm. David Adams, one of the latest sons of Penybanc was educated at Queen Elizabeth School at Carmarthen, took Holy orders and in 1665 emigrated to America. As a former president, Quincy Adams successfully supported slaves who had mutinied while being transported from Cuba.

THOMAS JEFFERSON

In his autobiography Thomas Jefferson says, 'The tradition in my father's family is that their ancestor came to this country from Wales, and from near the mountain of Snowdon. My father's estate on James River was called Snowdon after the supposed birthplace of the family.'

Parton the biographer said of Jefferson, 'Of all the public men in the United States he was incomparably the best scholar and most variously accomplished man'. We also know that Thomas Jefferson kept a Welsh dictionary in his library.

What's more, he named one of his horses Caractacus, the chieftain who led opposition to the Roman invasion of Britain. No man was ever more fond of his Welsh blood than he. He attended the William and Mary College and became a successful lawyer. He was elected President in 1801. It is claimed that the Declaration of Independence written by Jefferson was signed by 18 Welshmen or men partly of Welsh descent.

Thomas Jefferson

JAMES MONROE 1817-1825

His mother Elizabeth James Monroe is understood to have been of Welsh descent. According to his biographer she was the daughter of a well to do Welsh immigrant in King George County, Virginia.

WILLIAM HARRISON 1841

After just 31 days as the 9th president, he passed away from pneumonia, the first president to die in office. He had delivered the longest inaugural address in history at 1 hour 45 minutes. The story goes that he did so without a hat or coat during a snowstorm. The North America Wales Foundation lists him with roots in Wales, and it also lists James Madison and Calvin Coolidge.

ABRAHAM LINCOLN

Lincoln according to TA Glenn the New York historian was of Welsh descent on his mother's side and inherited her characteristics. His grandmother was Sarah Evans, daughter of Cadwallader Evans of Gwynedd Pennsylvania. He certainly understood the power of the Welsh in 19th century America. In 1860 he made a bid for the support of voters with roots in Wales by having up to 100,000 Welsh language election pamphlets printed.

JEFFERSON DAVIES

His great grandfather emigrated from Wales to Philadelphia, perhaps as early as 1701 when a number of Welsh Baptists landed in the Pennsylvania port. He served as a senator and secretary of war but left the Senate in 1861 when Mississippi where he had a cotton plantation seceded from the Union. He was captured and imprisoned for 2 years at the end of the Civil War. Jefferson Davies as well said he was the grandson of Evan Davies, youngest of 3 brothers who emigrated from Wales in the early part of the 18th century and who settled at Philadelphia. Jefferson became President of the Confederacy.

JAMES A GARFIELD

March 1881-September 1881

According to his 1881 biography, even as a boy the blood of his old Welsh ancestors was burning in his veins. In this account his mother tells him that the 1st James Garfield was one of the brave knights of Caerfili Castle. He became a major general during the Civil War on the Union side. He was shot by an embittered attorney who had sought a consular post and he died from his injuries.

RICHARD NIXON 1969-71

He is said to have been descended on his mother's side from the Pulleston family who lived at Hafod y Wern on what is now Wrexham Caia Estate. In the film 'Nixon' he was portrayed by one of Wales celebrated actors, Anthony Hopkins. Despite his role at Watergate, he did a lot to reconcile the United States with China.

Yale University owes its existence to a legacy of Elihu Yale who was born near Boston. He was the second son of David Yale, a native of Bryn Eglwys in which parish the manor house of Plas y Yale lies. Here the Yales lived for many generations.

William Penn once said to Hugh David a minister whom he knew, 'Hugh, I am a Welshman myself and I will tell you by how strange a circumstance our family lost our name. My grandfather was John Tudor and lived upon the top of a mountain or hill in Wales and was generally called John Penmynydd, which in English is John of the hilltop. He removed from Wales to Ireland where he acquired considerable property. Upon his return to his own country, he was addressed by his old friends and neighbours as Mr Penn, which became the family name.'

Rhodri Morgan AM once told me he was not popular with some of the Welsh because he was not keen on the Welsh language being the official language in the House of the Assembly. Other great Americans were Roger Williams who founded the State of Rhode Island, and JP Morgan the great banker.

Harvard University is greatly indebted to Joshua Mooney, a Welshman who collected funds for the institution. Brown University came into existence as a result of the efforts of Welsh ministers the Rev Morgan Edwards and Dr Samuel Jones.

Philips Academy was founded by a Welshman, Samuel Philips, and 2 other American institutions bear the names of their Welsh founders, Williams College and John Hopkins University.

Another great Welsh American was Frank Lloyd Wright, one of the world's top architects. It is interesting that the beginning of Carnegie's fortune was due to the extraordinary ability displayed by William R Jones in his management of Carnegie's new works at Braddock, near Pittsburg. The father of the anthracite iron trade of America was David Thomas, son of David and Jane Thomas of Tyllwyd Farm near Neath. He was regarded as an outstanding authority in all matters appertaining to the iron trade, and by his skill and industry to the building up of the iron industries of the country.

HILARY CLINTON

Hilary Clinton came from Welsh families on both sides and her father is buried in the Welsh cemetery at Scranton, PA. She was a recent contender for the US Presidency and is partner of ex-President Bill Clinton. She was a very able Secretary of State and has long been involved in American politics.

The Welsh have had a huge influence in the USA, with Hilary Clinton as the latest manifestation. Many of them were influential as industrial managers and many in the foundation of the state. Lately there has been some research which casts doubts on Jefferson's Welsh roots, but he certainly believed he had them.

THE SUFFRAGETTES

MARGARET HAIG THOMAS (LADY RHONDDA)

This only daughter of the immensely wealthy industrialist and politician DA Thomas and Sybil Haig Thomas of Llanwern was the secretary of the Newport branch of the suffragette Women's Social and Political Union. She was arrested after setting a letterbox alight in Newport. She smuggled her ammunition in a flimsy covered basket as she travelled home from London, - surely for the only time in her life - in a third-class railway carriage. Her arson attack was noticed and she was briefly imprisoned that summer.

She responded by going on hunger strike while in Usk Goal for her militant suffrage activity.

In 1926, the year of the General Strike, as a director of a number of coal companies, the strike had a big impact on Margaret, and her values of fairness.

During that year she was elected as the first sole female president of the Institute of Directors, a position she held for a decade. At this time, she became a key figure in the revival of pressure for extending the vote for all British women and she and Mrs Pankhurst (recently returned to London after running a teashop in the south of France) spoke at what proved to be the last mass demonstration in London for equal rights. Margaret chaired the group organising it and helped to orchestrate the activities that culminated in the equal franchise legislation of 1928.

Also, in 1926 she became editor of Time and Tide, the weekly review she had founded in 1920 and funded for the rest of her life. One of the most innovative, imaginative and adaptable of papers, it reflected the views of the newly enfranchised women over 30. She remained editor until her death in 1958.

In 1950 she became the first woman president of a Welsh college, the University College of South Wales and Monmouthshire, the forerunner of Cardiff University. For years she had advocated higher education as of huge importance to young women. She was a remarkable lady but had the good luck to be born into a very rich family and she used those riches wisely.

AMY DILLWYN

She was a cigar smoking cross dressing change maker, a trail blazing radical ahead of her time, a woman who became a legend in her lifetime. She was a bestselling novelist, pioneering industrialist, and campaigner for the rights of women and social justice. She wrote 6 novels, her themes included feminism, social reform, and a favourable view of the Rebecca Riots in response to unfair taxation. Following her father's death in 1892 Dillwyn inherited his spelter works at Llansamlet and his debts. She personally managed the industry and by 1899 had fully repaid her father's debts. In 1902 she turned her business into a registered company. She joined the National Union of Womens Suffrage Societies and continued campaigning for women's suffrage. She was presented at Queen Victoria's court as the daughter of a radical Swansea MP and friend of the Prince of Wales. She was never married, but considered herself married to a wife, Olive Talbot. She wore a bright purple skirt with a yellow rose in her belt and flowers in her hat at her father's funeral and was in general a flamboyant dresser. She was a great flag carrier for the women of Wales.

ROSEMARY CRAWSHAY

nee YEATES 1828 – 1907

Wife of Robert Thompson Crawshay who was buried at Vaynor churchyard with 'God Forgive Me' as his self-styled epitaph on his grave. She outlived her husband (they were married in May, 1846) by some twenty-five years, spending her latter years wintering on Lake Como in Italy.

She was her own person, a pioneer in many ways, starting up soup kitchens to feed the poor and contributing to a society in London to train girls ready for domestic service; she recognised the value of good literature and introduced prize schemes to encourage reading. The Rosemary Crawshay Prize in Literature is still being awarded to this day and she served as one of the first females on school governing bodies from 1871 onwards; she was a controversial supporter of the method at death of cremation; she was an early supporter and sympathiser of what became the suffragette cause (though she would not have been impressed by the increasing violence of the Pankhursts campaign from 1905 onwards) where she organised, chaired and spoke at the first suffrage meeting in Wales on 3rd June, 1870 at Merthyr Tydfil's Temperance Hall; vice president from the early 1970s for some thirty years of a suffrage organisation.

References:

Angela V John, *Rocking the Boat: Welsh Women Who Championed Equality 1840-1890* (Cardigan, Parthian 2018)

Angela V John, *Turning the Tide: The Life of Lady Rhondda* (Cardigan, Parthian 2013)

Ryland Wallace, *The Women's Suffrage Movement in Wales 1866-1928* (Cardiff, University of Wales Press 2009)

POLITICAL GIANTS OF THE 20TH CENTURY

JAMES KEIR HARDIE

The current leader of the Labour Party Sir Keir Starmers parents thought so much about Keir Hardie that they named their son after him.

Keir Hardie

In 1856, in a very small house in a Lanarkshire village, was born James Keir Hardie, a boy who was destined, when he grew up, to do a great deal for the workers of this and other countries, and thus win for himself world-wide fame. As a child he knew the bitterness of a poverty-stricken home, and when at only seven years old, he became the breadwinner for the family. Beginning as an errand boy, by the time he was 21 he had been a miner's trapper, pit-pony driver, and coal hewer. His mother had taught him to read, and the knowledge he acquired later by attending a night school, and by studying at home, enabled him to take a prominent part in local public affairs. The mining industry was in a deplorable condition at the time, and Keir Hardie appeared as the miner's representative before the masters. They consequently came to regard him as a 'labour agitator', and one day drove him and his brothers out of the pit.

A labour agitator he became, and he made himself independent of the masters by opening a stationery business and by doing journalistic work. He took the view that the miners should so organise their forces that they might secure for themselves direct and separate representation in Parliament instead of, as before, looking to the Liberals to protect their interests. In 1888, at a by-election in Mid-Lanarkshire, he appeared as an independent Labour candidate – the first of the kind in British politics. He was not elected, but his failure at the polls was followed by the formation of a Labour Party in Scotland, and great was the joy of the workers when in 1892 Keir Hardie entered Parliament as the Labour member for West Ham, a London constituency.

Keir Hardie's association with Merthyr Tydfil dates from 1898, the year of the long but unsuccessful miners' strike in South Wales. He addressed about 15 meetings in this district, and in the years that followed, the independent Labour Party made great strides in South Wales. At the General Election in 1900, though Keir Hardie came to the borough on the eve of the polling day and addressed two or three meetings only, he was elected as 'Junior Member for Merthyr.' The senior member was Mr DA Thomas, and these two men, one a strong Individualist and the other a confirmed Socialist, together represented Merthyr for 9 years. Keir Hardie continued to be the member for Merthyr Tydfil until his death in 1915.

Many and varied were his activities. Only passing reference can be made to his world-tour and his fearless opposition to the Great War, which he strove hard to avert, and of which he may be considered one of the victims. When he died it was largely from grief and disappointment, for he had cherished the hope that the workers of the various countries would unite as brothers and refuse to go to war with one another. He grieved that such a calamity as a world-war should have overtaken his fellow-men in this and other lands.

His work, however, was already done. Of the political parties in the land, the Labour Party owes its very existence to Keir Hardie, and it has already proved itself capable of maintaining the high traditions of a British Government. There had been few Labour members in the house of Commons in 1892, but he saw them grow in number until, in 1910, the working classes were directly represented by 42 members.

No man was ever more loyal to the people from whom he had sprung, nor better loved by them in return, and the workers of Merthyr Tydfil, therefore, are naturally proud to think that this great world figure was, for 15 years, known as 'Keir Hardie, the Junior Member for Merthyr.'

DAVID LLOYD GEORGE
1st EARL LLOYD-GEORGE OF DWYFOR (1863-1945)

'Conversation is not a monologue Winston!' David Lloyd George interrupting a lengthy one-sided discussion with Winston Churchill, quoted to the author by Lloyd George's daughter Jennifer Longford. David Lloyd George was the ultimate orator, the master of the one liner put down, even against esteemed orators such as Winston Churchill. It was this oratory that captivated those that both heard and read it. There are many books written both during and after David Lloyd George's lifetime. If these brief few words attract your interest, you are greatly encouraged to read some of them. It's hard to think of any British politician, with the possible exception of his lifetime friend Winston Churchill that left a longer lasting legacy both in the UK and across the world than David Lloyd George. It's also hard to think of any UK Prime Minister in the last few centuries beyond, David Lloyd George's (commonly known as LG) contemporary Ramsay MacDonald, who came from more humble origins and had a harder mountain to climb. Whereas his friend Winston Churchill was born in Blenheim Palace, LG was born in New York, New York Place, that is in Manchester. So there's the first surprise of LG's life story, the world's most famous Welsh politician was actually born in England.

David Lloyd George

His father (William George), however, in failing health returned to his Pembrokeshire farm, Haverfordwest three months after David's birth but died within 18 months. This left the infant David George, his young brother and sister on a journey away from the mainly English speaking south of Pembrokeshire to the informally Welsh speaking county of Caernarfonshire and the home of Elizabeth George's (LG's mother) brother Richard Lloyd. It was there in Llanystumdwy that Uncle Lloyd, the Anglican National School and a devout evangelical upbringing that shaped LG. He reflected this influence and would draw on his background and childhood amongst the 'common man' and their struggles throughout the rest of his career. Specifically, LG acknowledged the influence of his Uncle Lloyd both then and until he died in 1916 by adding the 'Lloyd' to his name to become David Lloyd George. To live in Wales in the late nineteenth century and to become part of the passion of rising Welsh nationalism and both middle and working class political struggles against the powers and dictate of the aristocracy, meant being a Liberal. Being an articled self-taught (through correspondence courses) solicitor who started his own practice in 1885 gave David the ability to both show his Liberal credentials in the court room and politically in the meeting halls.

He was initially a passionate advocate of Home Rule for Wales, the disestablishment of the Church in Wales (finally achieved when he was Prime Minister) and many other courses close to Welsh hearts. In January 1888 he married Margaret Owen, the daughter of a local prosperous farmer and between them they had five children, who both themselves and through their own offspring are still prominent today in academia, media and Westminster politics. Such was his own prominence that in April 1890 when a vacancy occurred for a by-election in the Caernarfon Borough's seat it was LG who won the seat from the Conservatives with a narrow 18 vote majority. He would hold the seat then until 1945, with ever larger majorities until it gained a Welsh record of 85.4 per cent in November 1918.

From his outset as a politician LG took on causes that were either mainly unpopular with the majority or with the ruling aristocracy and vested powers. These were either as a backbencher or in one of the many offices of state he held. In all

this time the 'Welsh Wizard' was never far from the national headlines. Thus his presence was felt across Wales and the world. He opposed the Boer War (popular with a jingoistic public at the time and something that frequently endangered his own life.)

He opposed and led a rebellion against the Education Act 1902, which sought to make Welsh Nonconformist rate payers pay for Church of England schools. He introduced the welfare state, including Old Age Pensions (which were even called Lloyd Georges for a time) and National Insurance, which was not popular with the wealthy and landed aristocracy who were made to pay for part of the cost.

He introduced the Welsh Church Act 1914, which removed much of the power and privilege of the Church of England in Wales, which was not popular with the bishops. LG was the dynamo behind much of the activity which both led to him becoming Prime Minister and eventually helping to win the First World War. This was through measures such as conscription, introducing the convoy system at sea, taxing people higher than ever before, regulating their lives, rationing and censorship, directing industrial relations and nationalising the economy more than ever before. LG reduced the opening hours of pubs and legally watered down the beer. LG was also particularly unpopular with numerous generals with whom he frequently clashed over their often bloodthirsty battle tactics. LG was, however, popular enough with both the nation and the Conservative opposition to become Prime Minister in 1916 in something of a palace coup, which removed his predecessor HH Asquith and subsequently split the Liberal Party in two with an Asquith and LG grouping.

Whilst being the post war Prime Minister, LG tackled problems the like of which no other UK Prime Minister had in such a combination. Demobilising and putting back into the workforce millions of servicemen, tackling the decline of the staple industries of coal, steel and ship building, plus the Spanish flu. Internationally

33

the collapse of the national and European economies and nation states, partially dealt with unsuccessfully at the Treaty of Versailles, the civil war and partition of Ireland, the redrawing of the boundaries of the Middle east and establishment of Palestine, the Russian Revolution, a pending war between Greece and Turkey and the preservation of the still expanding British Empire. This was done at the same time as holding together a coalition government that was mainly Conservative and had become increasingly hostile at its grass roots level to being led by LG. This latter fact led directly to the Conservatives withdrawing from the coalition arrangement, LG ceasing to be Prime Minister in October 1922 and never regaining a national office again. In his private life, although they were married until she died in 1941, his relationship with Dame Margaret (the most famous Welsh political woman of her era) was not the only woman he had a relationship with. Far from it. Today LG is as famous for his extra martial affairs in the public's eye as anything else he did, even being 'the man who won the (First World) war!'. Whole books have been written about the many women in LGs life, most notably Ffion Hagues The Pain and the Privilege. LG it could be said enjoyed a partial polyamorous relationship at times, with both his wife and mistresses being aware of his relationship with each other and passively consenting to it for much of the time. But the relationships did not end there. In fact, such were his powers of seduction that Jennifer Longford (LGs daughter from his second wife), once told this author that they would not employ any woman to work with LG under the age of her mid 50s. One of those previously seduced was his Private Secretary, whilst he was Prime Minister, Frances Stevenson, who after Dame Margaret died became his second wife and the keeper of the LG legacy flame until her own death in 1972. She was 23 years his junior and the same age as his daughter Mair, who had died of appendicitis when she was only 17.

On the political front, as well, LG was tormented and later supported by the women's suffrage movement. Initially a target for their radicalism he later worked with them on getting them accepted to the labour force during the First World War and allowing women to demonstrate that they were equal to men across many sectors of

34

society, which in turn led to him being the Prime Minister who enabled women to vote wholesale for the first time and stand for office at Westminster in 1918 (albeit it at the age of 30 compared to 21 for men with respect to voting).

Lloyd George is seen today as something of a disappointment in many Welsh nationalists' eyes. He failed to establish a Welsh Parliament, something he had been so passionately behind (Home Rule for Wales) earlier on in his career. This was seen then and now as a betrayal for Wales. Yet at the same time both before and whilst he was Prime Minister he helped or directly introduced many of the trappings of Welsh nationhood.

He helped ensure the establishment of the National Library and Museums of Wales, established Welsh regiments like the Guards, enabled them to wear the Welsh dragon on the Welsh regiments uniforms and ensured that the daffodil was once again seen as the national symbol of Wales, wearing it at the Investiture of the Prince of Wales in Caernarfon in 1911, another event seen world wide which boosted the status of Wales. LG saw himself, foremost as being Welsh, employed a Welsh speaking staff in Downing Street and supported Welsh and religious life both in Wales and elsewhere ranging from the London Welsh speaking church (The Welsh Baptist Chapel) to attending and speaking at the various National Eisteddfods.

He ensured his first family with Dame Margaret were all Welsh speakers and that was the language they used first and foremost. Although he lived much of his life in England he always retained a residency in Caernarfonshire and it was here that he moved to for his final resting place (where today you can find the Lloyd George Museum). That Museum is also perhaps a fitting place for one to visit to see something more of the whole story of the most clearly Welsh figure ever to lead a government in the United Kingdom.

Lloyd George's Secretary was Dr Thomas Jones (1870-1955) When they were negotiating the Anglo-Irish Treaty in 1921, Michael Collins would speak to the other Irish delegates in Gaelic; Jones would then turn to Lloyd George and speak in Welsh. Born in 1870

Dr Thomas Jones, better known as "TJ", may well be one of the most prominent Welshman in politics in the first half of the twentieth century that you may never have heard of.

As Deputy Secretary to four Prime Ministers during the First World War and inter-war period he was often both an essential source of advice and a confidante. The son of a Welsh speaking family from Rhymney he was the first of nine children and enjoyed an education at the prestigious Lewis School, Pengam. Having decided to study for the Ministry via University College of Wales Aberystwyth he then had a change of direction and went to the University of Glasgow to study economics, something that would lead to him becoming Professor of Economics at Queen's University, Belfast in 1909. Although Aberystwyth didn't provide him with a vocation it did provide him with a wife, as it was there that he met and later married Eirene Theodora Lloyd. TJ returned to Wales in 1910 and became Secretary of the Welsh National Campaign against Tuberculosis and then holding the same post on the National Health Insurance Commission (Wales).

His exceptional drive and energy became known to a man sharing these same virtues, David Lloyd George, which in turn helped get him to play a central role in the War Cabinet Secretariat. During that period as TJ noted himself in his extensive diaries: 'Our common Welsh background and our mutual use of the language made intimate relations with Lloyd George easy, and I was welcomed at the famous breakfasts and used on confidential errands to and from his colleagues'.

He then played a similar role for the next three Prime Ministers, both Conservative and Labour/National. Being at the heart of helping on foreign and domestic policy ranging from the winning of the First World War, the General Strike of 1926, the Great Depression and the Irish Treaty to the Russian Revolution, potential war between Greece and Turkey to the attempts to improve Anglo-German relations in the 1930s.

As well as being influential on British domestic and international policy TJ played a prominent part in the development of Welsh cultural and educational life. Although he had grave reservations about Welsh political nationalism he was one of the founders and first editor of the political and cultural magazine The Welsh Outlook, funded by his friend Lord Davies. Similarly he was the principal founder of the Welsh adult college Coleg Harlech and Gregynog Press.

His drive was also harnessed on Welsh University councils, and as President of both the National Library and Museum of Wales as well as numerous Welsh charitable trusts. An accomplished author his best work is undoubtedly his three volumes of the Whitehall Diaries, which provide us with both a candid and vivid portrait of what life was like at the centre of power during the interwar years and how government really operated. A story seen through the eyes of a man who was also known as 'the King of Wales, keeper of a thousand secrets' and like his friend and the man he served, Lloyd George, someone who helped build up the cultural and educational fabric of the nation he called home - Wales.

This essay is by Professor Russell Deacon (Chairman of the Lloyd George Society)

Further reading: J Graham Jones, Gwilym Lloyd-George, first Viscount Tenby (1894-1967) in *David Lloyd George and Welsh Liberalism*, Welsh Political Archive, National Library of Wales, 2010 Kenneth O Morgan, Gwilym Lloyd-George, first Viscount Tenby, Oxford Dictionary of National Biography, online version 6 January 2011 Paul Ward, Gwilym Lloyd-George (1894-1967): Welsh National and British State in Unionism in the United Kingdom, 1918-1974, Palgrave Macmillan, 2005 Merfyn Jones, *A Radical Life*: The Biography of Megan Lloyd George, Hutchinson, 1991 Paul Ward, Megan Lloyd George (1902-1966) Welsh Radical: in Welsh National and British State in Unionism in the United Kingdom Kirsty Williams, Lady Megan Lloyd George in *The Honourable Ladies*, Volume I; Iain Dale and Jacqui Smith (eds.) Biteback publications, 2018.

GWILYM AND MEGAN LLOYD GEORGE

By Graham Lippiatt

Graham Lippiatt is a Contributing Editor to the Journal of Liberal History and Secretary of the Lloyd George Society

Gwilym and Megan Lloyd George: the multi-party politics of the Lloyd George children Gwilym Lloyd-George (1894-1967) and Megan Lloyd George (1902-1966) followed their father into Parliament as Liberal MPs in 1922 and 1929 respectively. But neither ended their political careers in the Liberal Party. Their father predicted as much. On 14 April 1938 L.G.'s principal private secretary, A J Sylvester, noted in his diary that 'L. G. thinks that Gwilym will go to the right and Megan to the left, eventually.' And, in the end, Gwilym became a Conservative and Megan defected to Labour. Both Gwilym and Megan Lloyd

Megan Lloyd George

38

George made important contributions to Welsh political history, both believing that their paths followed the ideals of their father. Both retained their Welsh identity, not least through their relationship with their mother, Margaret Lloyd George, who spent most of her life in North Wales; and their Welshness was linked as greatly to their political careers as to their personal lives. Megan famously was the first woman ever to win a Parliamentary seat in Wales when she became MP for Anglesey at the 1929 General Election. In 1954 Gwilym was the first Welshman appointed as Minister for Welsh Affairs – the office which was later upgraded to Minister of State and eventually Secretary of State. Gwilym Lloyd-George:

Born in Criccieth, Gwilym followed his fathers path from a distinctly Welsh to a more British identity. David Lloyd George did this through his rise from fiery backbencher to Downing Street and international politics. For Gwilym it was acquired through his education at Eastbourne College and Cambridge, his active service in France during the Great War and the congeniality of the House of Commons. Like his father, however, he never relinquished his love of Wales and a belief in its separateness as a nation. Gwilym entered Parliament as Liberal

MP for Pembrokeshire at the General Election of 1922 in a straight fight against Labour. The local Conservatives had decided to support Gwilym as the anti-socialist candidate. Throughout his career Gwilym remained a committed antisocialist and like his father believed there was a distinct boundary between Liberal radicalism and state interventionist socialism. Gwilym held Pembrokeshire at the 1923 election, now against Conservative as well as Labour opponents, giving prominence in his campaign to radical new Liberal land policies but lost in 1924. While out of Parliament Gwilym worked for his fathers newspapers and helped in the development of new policies for industry and the land, as well as becoming a Trustee of the notorious Lloyd George Fund.

In 1929 he regained Pembrokeshire and held the seat until defeated in the 1950 General Election. He served briefly at the Board of Trade under the National Government but refused to give up his belief in Free Trade and resigned over proposals to impose tariffs. He remained part of the small Lloyd George family group in Parliament during this time. David Lloyd Georges speech during the Norway Debate of 1940 was a factor in Churchills installation as Prime Minister and Gwilym supported the wartime coalition, serving as a junior minister at the Board of Trade and Ministry of Food and after 1942 as Minister of Fuel and Power working closely with Ernest Bevin on the 'Bevin Boys' scheme to increase the labour force in the mines.

When the war ended he remained a member of the government and was re-elected in Pembrokeshire as a National Liberal and Conservative, his increasingly British identity and committed anti-socialism helping to ease his path towards the Tories. After 1945 he was offered the leadership of both Liberal and National Liberal parties but rejected both.

In 1950 he lost Pembrokeshire to Labour but was quickly re-elected as a National Liberal and Conservative for Newcastle upon Tyne North in 1951, holding the seat in 1955. By now having added a hyphen to his surname, Gwilym served as Minister of Food from 1951-1954 overseeing the end of rationing. He then became Home Secretary which included responsibility as Minister for Welsh Affairs. During this time the Parliament for Wales Campaign was active and there was a Private Members Bill calling for Welsh Home Rule. Gwilym re-asserted his belief in the separateness of Welsh identity and nationhood but never supported the idea of Welsh independence. 'The vitality of the Welsh nation', he declared, 'can be better preserved if the Welsh people remain within the framework of Great Britain'. In 1955 Gwilym was elevated to the peerage as Lord Tenby.

Megan Lloyd George had a different, closer, relationship with her father than Gwilym did. She was educated at home, including at Downing Street and it was David Lloyd George, his radicalism, his Welsh identity and as Megan saw it, his Welsh nationalism, which defined Megan's view of politics throughout her career.

In 1929 Megan Lloyd George became the first woman to represent a Welsh constituency in Parliament when she won the Anglesey seat at the General Election. Anglesey was an essentially poor, rural seat close to her father's Caernarfon Boroughs, where over 80% of the population spoke Welsh. Megan held the seat until 1951, when it went Labour. Unlike her brother, Megan never served in government but used her campaigning and oratorical skills to pursue the radical agenda she associated with her father.

Her maiden speech in the House she used to highlight the plight of rural housing and spoke regularly on agriculture, unemployment and often on other issues affecting Wales and Welshness. Megan also stuck closely to her father during the period of the National government and she strongly supported David Lloyd George's policies on unemployment during the 1935 election campaign. Like Gwilym, Megan also went to Germany with her father in 1936. Perhaps crucially she was instrumental in persuading her father to come to the floor of the Commons and make his speech in the Norway Debate. Increasingly during the 1940s, as her father's health deteriorated and his powers faded, Megans Welshness was exerting an influence and she was increasingly drawn to campaigns reflecting her father's old support for Cymru Fydd. In 1938 and 1944, arguing for better representation for Wales at government level, she was a member of deputations to Downing Street calling for the creation of a Secretary of State for Wales.

Again in 1944, in her role as Chairman of the Welsh Parliamentary Party, she secured the 'Welsh Day' of debates in the House of Commons. Megan supported the creation of the Parliament for Wales Campaign in the late 1940s and was appointed its president. The campaign called for Welsh self-government within the framework of the United Kingdom. However most other Welsh MPs failed to support it and devolution remained a minority movement until much later. Megan pursued other radical causes echoing the past campaigns of her father.

During the Second World War she served on consultative committees on health, labour and National Service. She argued for electoral reform and campaigned for issues around the employment

41

of women and womens rights. She was also associated during this time with the internal Liberal party ginger group, Radical Action, which questioned the need for the wartime electoral truce, campaigned for the Beveridge Report and championed the independence of the Liberal Party over the coalition government. After the war it prioritised social liberal ideas at a time when the party seemed to be captured by economic liberal thinking. Megan believed that the Liberal Party under Clement Davies after 1945 was pulling it inexorably to the right.

Despite her acceptance of the deputy leadership of the party, Megans radicalism was exerting a pull towards cooperation with Labour. After losing her Anglesey seat in 1951, Megan declined the chance to stand there again for the Liberals and eventually joined Labour in April 1955, proclaiming that party had inherited the mantle of the Welsh Radical tradition from the Liberals. Perhaps Megans turn to Labour was helped by her long-term relationship with Labour politician Philip Noel-Baker but a number of other Liberal figures including Dingle Foot and Tom Horabin also left the party for Labour at this time amid internal concern over Davies' leadership.

In 1957 Megan was adopted as the Labour candidate for Carmarthen and defeated the Liberals in their own seat at a by-election. In Parliament Megan continued to speak on Welsh matters but never held front bench office under Labour. She died in 1966.

Somewhat ironically perhaps, the subsequent by-election in her seat was won by Plaid Cymru. So, while Gwilym drifted right and Megan left, as their father had predicted, they both in their own ways stayed true to the national feeling and radical politics inherited from David Lloyd George. At a time of realignment in British politics their two political journeys mirror the decline of the Liberal Party and the search by former Liberals for a place in politics which represented a link with their past beliefs and a vehicle through which these traditions could be progressed.

Further reading: J Graham Jones, Gwilym Lloyd-George, first Viscount Tenby (1894-1967) in *David Lloyd George and Welsh Liberalism*, Welsh Political Archive, National Library of Wales, 2010 Kenneth O Morgan, Gwilym Lloyd-George, first Viscount Tenby, Oxford Dictionary of National Biography, online version January 2011 Paul Ward, Gwilym Lloyd-George (1894-1967): Welsh National and British State in Unionism in the United Kingdom, 1918-1974, Palgrave Macmillan, 2005 Merfyn Jones, *A Radical Life: The Biography of Megan Lloyd George*, Hutchinson, 1991 Paul Ward, Megan Lloyd George (1902-1966) Welsh Radical: in Welsh National and British State in Unionism in the United Kingdom Kirsty Williams, Lady Megan Lloyd George in *The Honourable Ladies*, Volume I; Iain Dale and Jacqui Smith (eds.) Biteback publications, 2018.

GWENLLIAN MORGAN

She died on 7th November 1939 aged 87.

The mayor at the time said, 'A great light has been extinguished'. She had become the first Welsh woman councillor; she was a philanthropist, educationalist, magistrate, historian of exceptional brilliance, writer of no mean ability, and recognised far and wide as an authority of the highest order on antiquities.

She was not only the first woman town councillor in Wales, she was also the first woman in the Principality to serve the office of mayor and she was the first 'friend' of Brecon Cathedral. Her ancestors had held land and property at Defynnog for over 300 years.

It was a hard world for those with small incomes, and Gwenllian Morgan was aware of it. All the same, she had no time for layabouts and gave them short shrift. To those that were sick, to the old ladies in the alms-houses and to the young children in the Poor Law Institution she gave extra kindness. She was a governor of the Brecon County schools, a Poor Law guardian, and she was also a member of the Joint Advisory Committee of the National Health Insurance, a governor of the Edward Vll National Memorial, chairman of the

Breconshire Association of Friendly Societies and a magistrate.

The Morgan family were staunch Liberals. Gwenllian was a woman of great gifts of mind and character and was an eloquent speaker with a striking command of the English language. She had a natural love of study and research. She did come in for some prejudice on election into local government. The manner in which she carried out the mayoral duties in an important Coronation year impressed Breconians more than ever. Her portrait was given to the Guildhall in Brecon and it is said she had been a valuable member of the Brecon Education Committee and she was always ready to promote true religious morality, purity and peace, thrift, cleanliness and health.

She was presented with an album containing an illuminated address to her with the names of 920 female subscribers. It was a great evening for Brecon when Lord and Lady Glanusk gave her the presentations.

On the various spheres in which she had been successful it is difficult to put one before the other. A subject close to her heart was Henry Vaughan the Breconshire poet. Her thorough research resulted in the gathering of a vast amount of material. On the afternoon of 21st July 1925, the University of Wales conferred upon Gwenllian Morgan the Honorary Degree of MA in recognition of her research into the life of Vaughan. Books on Vaughan have increased in recent years just as his works are becoming known in every part of the English-speaking world. There can be little doubt that the writings of Gwenllian Morgan are a most valuable contribution to this most famous Breconshire man. In 1920 she was appointed church warden of the Priory Church, an appointment she held until 1922.

She was a woman of huge quality who made a marvellous contribution to her home town of Brecon.

There is a large housing court in Brecon named after her and she is still remembered fondly by the town.

THE GALLANT MEMBERS

MAJOR GENERAL IVOR PHILIPPS

MAMETZ WOOD

By Chris Thomas MA

While Wales produced some of the United Kingdom's most famous political personalities of the 20th Century, two of the less high-profile Welsh politicians who were to achieve considerable success in the world of business and finance are the Philipps brothers, John and Ivor. This chapter is indebted to the excellent work Business success and the role of chance the extraordinary Philipps brothers by P.N. Davies and the bibliographic research of David Lewis Jones in Y Bywgraffiadur Cymraeg (The Dictionary of Welsh Biography) which provides some of the content which follows. In addition, the findings of recent research by this Chapter's author in the parliamentary archives at Westminster and the National Library of Wales substantiates findings which redress some of the popular misconceptions about the military career of Ivor Philipps and his command of the 38th (Welsh) Division in the First World War.

Davies noted Burke's Peerage which identifies the Philipps' as an ancient Welsh family tracing its lineage back to Cadifor ap Collwyn, Lord of Dyvett in the 11th Century. He went on to say that family tradition suggested that their ancestry could be traced back via successive Princes of Dyfed to AD50. Bledri Latimer for instance, was one of a number of family members who held high office, having been made Lord Justice of South Wales through homage to Henry II. His descendant Sir Aron ap Rees further increased his family's influence in high circles by accompanying King Richard Coeur de Lion on the Crusade to the Holy Land in 1190. While serving there, he was awarded the 'Order of Knighthood of the Sepulchre of Our Saviour' for making his pilgrimage to the holy lands. Over the next seven hundred and fifty hundred, years the family continued to hold both high office and positions of influence. The marriage of Sir Thomas Philipps to Jane, daughter and co-heir of Henry Doune brought considerable additional lands in South Wales into the family which included Picton Castle. It subsequently became the family seat from which the then John Philipps, MP for Pembroke was created a Baronet in 1621. In 1766, the 7th Baronet Sir Richard Philipps was raised to the peerage as Lord Milford, although the title was lost when he died without a male heir.

John and Ivor Philipps were the eldest of six sons and five daughters. Their father was Sir James Erasmus Philipps, Vicar of Warminster and later Prebendary of Salisbury Cathedral. He was the holder of the hereditary baronetcy which John later inherited as the thirteenth Baronet. As was seen in the lineage of their ancestors, politics and influence in high places was to be found in the life and careers of both John and Ivor. Educated at Felstead School they were to pursue different careers after they completed their secondary education, although their paths probably crossed many times in both the political and business worlds.

After Felstead, John studied Modern History at Keble College Oxford while Ivor pursued a career in the Army. Soon after his marriage to Leonora Gerstenberg in 1888, John entered politics as the Liberal Member of Parliament for Mid-Lanarkshire, a post he held for six years before following family tradition and returning to Pembrokeshire as Member of Parliament for the constituency until he was raised to the peerage as Baron St Davids in 1898. Davies noted that from the time of his marriage to Leonora, John's business interests grew exponentially in the field of Investment Trusts. He founded the Premier Investment Company in 1892 and joined the Consolidated Trust as a Director. In later years, 'John... also joined the boards of both the Municipal Trust Company and the International Financial Society and... by 1914 had become the lynchpin of the '69, Old Broad Street Group', which at that time through interlocking directorships managed a number of Trusts as well as Government Stock'. John also developed extensive commercial interests in shipping and railway transport particularly in

South America through the Argentine Great Western, the Buenos Aires and Pacific and the Costa Rica Railway Companies among others. Further recognition of his achievements came in 1922 in his appointment as a Knight Grand Cross of the Order of the British Empire. He also became Lord Lieutenant of Pembrokeshire, a post he held until 1932. He died aged 77 in 1938.

When John and Ivor parted ways after their education at Felstead, Ivor joined the Wiltshire Militia in 1881 and was subsequently commissioned into the Manchester Regiment in 1883, which at that time was based in India. In 1884 he transferred to the 1st Battalion, 5th Gurkha Regiment. It heralded a successful military career. Davies noted:

'He saw active service in the Burma campaign of 1887-89, for which he received the medal and two clasps. Next he took part in the Chin Lushi Expedition in 1889, and two years later was awarded a clasp for his participation in the Miranzai expedition. In 1892 he served with the Isazai expedition and in 1896 the part he played on the North-West Frontier earned for him the medal and two clasps. He distinguished himself in the Tirah Campaign of 1896-7 for which he received a further clasp, his services being mentioned twice in dispatches.'

Having demonstrated what Jones described as 'considerable administrative gifts', Philipps was appointed Deputy Assistant Adjutant and Quarter Master General of the British force sent to rescue the besieged legations in Beijing during the China Expedition of 1900-01. He was awarded the Distinguished Service Order and mentioned in Dispatches twice for his services, retiring from the Indian Army in 1903 as a Major. Shortly thereafter he joined the Pembroke Yeomanry and was promoted to Lieutenant-Colonel as the regiment's commanding officer in 1908, eventually retiring from military service in 1912. His command was concurrent with his tenure as a Liberal Member of Parliament for Southampton until losing his seat at the General Election of 1922.

More significant than the active service and administrative

experience that Philipps had amassed during 20 years in the regular army, was the career he forged in business between 1903 and 1914. From the time Ivor became Chairman of the Baku Russian Oil Company which he joined in 1905 at the behest of his brother John, his own business network grew considerably to the extent that by 1912 he was chairman in seven of the fourteen companies in which he held directorships. Clearly possessing considerable business acumen he was elected to the board of the ailing Schweppes company in February 1914. Simmons noted, 'As sometimes happens in history, the hour of need produced for the company a leader with the right qualities... Ivor unhesitatingly set about his task'. Clearly not a man to shirk difficult issues, tough decisions and, seeing himself as something of a reformer, his business experience immediately led him to restructure the company's shareholder dividend payment scheme to improve the company's financial position. The outbreak of war brought Ivor back to the colours as a Staff Officer at the Ministry of War while retaining his seat in Parliament. He was quickly promoted to Brigadier-General when appointed to raise the third Brigade of the Welsh Army Corps – more commonly known at the time as 'Lloyd George's Welsh Army'.

Whilst appearing to conflict with national policy for recruitment into the regular and territorial army in the early years of the war, the Welsh Army Corps principal raison d'etre was recruitment in Wales to feed the insatiable appetite of Britain's war effort. By 18 November 1914, three brigades had been established with headquarters in Llandudno, Rhyl and Colwyn Bay where 3 Brigade was based with Philipps as its commanding officer. By Christmas 1914 the estimated strength of the Corps was 10,000 men which included artillery, engineer, signal and medical services.

Typical of the Corps make-do approach to training, Hughes observed that the artillery had no guns but practised limbering up using pairs of old bus wheels fastened to long poles. With untrained troops scattered across Wales, it was soon evident that the Corps was an amateurish, disparate and decentralised organisation, lacking in coordination and faced with the challenge of turning enthusiastic recruits into trained soldiers, ready and committed to face the highly trained armies of the continental powers.

The wellbeing of the Corps was a serious issue that demanded swift remedies, prompting a flurry of action and correspondence between Ivor, Lloyd George and Kitchener during late December 1914 and January 1915. Lloyd George confirmed to Ivor on 7 January that he had written 'a very strong letter to Kitchener', subsequently meeting with him to discuss the matter of Ivor taking command of the Corps. The outcome was that Kitchener promised to meet with Ivor to talk the matter over. However, matters were not resolved quickly, prompting Ivor to write again to Lloyd George on 17 January from his headquarters of 3 Brigade at Colwyn Bay:

'I am very anxious to hear the result of your last interview with Lord Kitchener, as every day I become more convinced of the urgent necessity for the appointment of some military head to your Welsh Army Corps. At present there is no-one specially entrusted with the important work of coordinating the efforts of all the brigade commanders, the recruiting agencies and the Welsh Army Corps committee. I am sure much more could be done if the committee had one military officer to advise and help them.'

Lloyd George's persuasive powers prevailed and he confirmed to Ivor, 'This morning I saw K and got him to issue the order before I left the room for Gazetting you as divisional commander… it will appear in the next issue of the Gazette.' The Armys Western Command confirmed Ivors appointment as a Major-General, and by 20 January, he had formally received his orders from the War Office to take command of what was then designated the 43rd Welsh Division and later renamed the 38th (Welsh) Division. By way of thanks for his appointment, Ivor wrote to Lloyd George confirming that 'I have written to your second son… I propose to offer him a post on my staff as Aide de Camp which I hope will suit him. I am sure he will be of use to me'.

As well as being the General Officer Commanding the 43rd Division, Ivor also continued with his responsibilities at the War

Office, specifically in the Ministry of Munitions as Military Secretary. As such, he was involved in the 'Big Gun Programme' whose objective was to increase the Army's heavy artillery formations. He was also involved in other vital work to remedy the massive inefficiencies in the British munitions manufacturing industry which produced significant numbers of 'dud' shells for the Western Front in the early years of the war.

Correspondence also shows that he was involved in inter-army liaison with the French, specifically with General Gossot from French high command - Grand Quartier Général - with whom Ivor was corresponding up to October 1915. Gossot is identified by Lloyd George as being part of a French army delegation at a meeting in Boulogne in June 1915, although it is not clear if Ivor was also present. From Lloyd Georges correspondence, it is clear that Ivor's contribution to the work of the Ministry of Munitions as Military Secretary was of considerable value. Lloyd George commented, 'You know what difficulties and perplexities we have had to face, and if they have now been to a great extent overcome, it has been largely due to the energy, the business capacity, the tact and loyalty which you have invariably shown.'

As a senior British officer during the First World War, Ivor Philipps is a character who has been much neglected by military historians and maligned by his regular army counterparts of the time. He has been portrayed by some as the man largely responsible for the for 38th (Welsh) Division's difficulties and high casualty rates at the Battle of Mametz Wood in July 1916. In their eyes, his only apparent claim to fame was to be removed from post during the battle for the Division's lack of effectiveness. Consequently, it has been easy for scholarship to categorise him alongside the many incompetent senior British commanders. However, closer examination of the individual through the author's own research, his professional abilities and contribution to the British war effort presents a rather different picture to the one that scholarship has perhaps inadvertently created by focussing solely on the negative aspects of First World War command and leadership.

With regard to the performance of 38th (Welsh) Division at the Battle of Mametz Wood, evidence clearly shows that Ivor's immediate superior in July 1916, General Henry Horne, effectively hamstrung his decision making abilities by countermanding Ivor's planning by issuing inflexible and wholly inappropriate orders from XV Corps command. On Horne's part it demonstrated little tactical appreciation of the battle landscape at Mametz Wood during the actions of 7-12th July 1916. It was Hornes orders that were almost exclusively responsible for the devastating casualties suffered by 38th Division on the first day of the battle. That same man went on to command the British First Army by the end of the war.

That said, Ivor was knighted in 1917 for services to the British war effort and post-war returned to his position as Chairman of Schweppes guiding it in its highly successful global expansion programme, whilst also becoming a director and chairman of a number of other companies which included the British Industries and General Investment Trust, Ilford, British Alkaloids, Kia-Ora as well as the World Marine and General Insurance companies.

Davies noted, 'Needless to say there are many links between some of these firms and those controlled by other members of his family and it would appear to be unlikely that without their support – particularly from John Philipps – that he would have been unable to make such rapid progress'.

The inter-war years saw Ivor serve as Alderman of Pembroke as well as Deputy and Vice-Lieutenant for the County of Pembrokeshire. Davies noted that he 'put considerable effort into the restoration of Pembroke Castle… after it had come into his possession in 1928 and was given the Freedom of the Borough for his work in 1936. Ivor died on 16 August 1940, two years after his brother John, leaving behind them many years of distinguished public and military service and considerable commercial success.

Bibliography

Primary Sources

 Imperial War museum

 National Archives

 National Army Museum

 National Library of Wales

 United Kingdom Parliament Archives

Secondary Sources

 Davies, PN, "Business success and the role of chance the extraordinary Philipps brothers", Business

 History, 23, 2, 1981.

 Howell, RL and Meyrick, TF, History of the Pembroke Yeomanry, (Published by the Pembroke Yeomanry, 1959).

 Hughes, Colin, Mametz, (Place of publication not identified: Gliddon Books, 1990).

 Jones, David, "Phillips, Sir Ivor (1861-1940): Soldier, Politician and Businessman", Dictionary of Welsh Biography, https://biography.wales/article

 Lloyd George, David, War Memoirs of David Lloyd George, (London: Odhams Press, 1938).

 Report of the Executive Committee, Welsh Army Corps 1914-1919, (Cardiff: Western Mail, 1921).

 Simmons Douglas, Schweppes, The First 200 Years, (London: Springwood Books, 1983).

 Thomas, Christopher, "An evaluation of command effectiveness in the British Expeditionary Force using the early twentieth-century business management theories of the French industrialist Henri Fayol as tools to interrogate the Axes of Command in the 38 (Welsh) Division, its 113 Brigade and XV Corps, 1914-1916". University of Birmingham, Masters in Military History Dissertation, September 2021.

LORD PETER THOMAS QC

Thomas was born in Llanrwst in July 1920. He was educated at the village school and then at Epworth College in Rhyl, before reading law at Jesus College Oxford. He joined the Royal Air Force in 1939 on the outbreak of WW2. He was shot down while serving as a bomber pilot in 1941 and spent 4 years in prisoner of war camps in Germany. This is where he met the author's father who directed him as one of the leading ladies in the prisoners pantomime!

He became a barrister after the war and was called to the Bar in 1947 at Middle Temple. He practised on the Wales and Chester circuit and took Silk in 1965. He was bilingual in Welsh and English and took an active part in the Gorsedd (National Eisteddfod) Whilst at Jesus he joined the Conservative Association. In 1950 he was elected for his birthplace, Conway, winning it in 1951 by a slim majority.

He was a tall man with rugged beaky good looks and wavy grey hair. His easy charm and breezy extrovert warmth won him many friends, including Labour's Lord Cledwyn who shared his North Wales origins. His only impediment was a hearing difficulty. After being Edward Heath's Conservative Party chairman in 1970-72 he became the Minister for Wales throughout Heath's government 1970-74. He was in the forefront for demands for Welsh autonomy, urging a separate Welsh office as a halfway house to a Welsh Parliament as early as 1957.

His loyalty to Heath prompted him to resign from the Shadow Cabinet in 1975, as soon as Margaret Thatcher became leader. To start off with he didn't favour her, but eventually came over to her side, applauding her as a remarkable person. During the whole of Edward Heath's Premiership Thomas held the position of Secretary of State for Wales. He was Secretary of State during a period of violent activism by those promoting the Welsh language, including bombings and the campaign by the Welsh Language Society to remove English road signs. He dealt with this tactfully. He remained a fervent Zionist and backed the War Crimes bill against the majority of Tory peers after he'd entered The Lords. He backed Lord Crickhowell's bill to build the Cardiff Bay barrage because that deprived area required regeneration. He was a great supporter of Mikhail Gorbachev's and described his contributions to peace as greater than those of any other 20th century foreign leader.

He was an excellent and distinguished Secretary of State for Wales.

DAVID GIBSON- WATT MC PC

Baron Gibson-Watt of the Wye in the District of Radnor (1921-2002)

By James Gibson-Watt. Leader of Powys County Council

David Gibson-Watt

The life of David Gibson-Watt would certainly deserve to be described as 'distinguished' even without including his military service; but once one includes that, he is revealed as one of the most extraordinary Welshmen of the 20th Century. A direct descendant of the 'father of the Industrial Revolution' James Watt and the leading classical economist David Ricardo, he was born in September 1918 and raised on the extensive farming and forestry estate near

55

Llandrindod Wells in Mid Wales first established by James Watt in the early 19th Century. Educated at Eton and Trinity College, Cambridge, in October 1939 he was commissioned into the Welsh Guards. He served throughout the Second World War and during the North African campaign. As commander of No. 4 Company, 3rd Battalion, Welsh Guards, Gibson- Watt was ordered to take part in the attack, in May 1943, on the town of Hamman- Lif, Tunisia.

Although wounded during the advance, he continued to lead his men throughout a ferocious engagement. As a result, he was awarded his first Military Cross for outstanding gallantry and leadership. Later, in early 1944 during the Italian campaign, Gibson- Watt took part in the defence of Monte Cerasola, near Monte Cassino, and his conduct during a successful counter- attack on 9 February earned him the award of a Bar to his Military Cross. Two months later, he led No. 4 Company in an attack across the River Po as the Allied armies advanced north and was awarded a second Bar for his inspiring leadership and almost reckless courage. To those who knew him, that display of 'almost reckless courage' in leading his men would come as no surprise, as throughout his life his constant concern for others and almost complete absence of concern for himself were a key feature of his personality.

He achieved the rank of Major and became an instructor at Sandhurst after the War before leaving the Army in 1946, initially to return to his home and apply himself to the care of his family's estate and the many farmers and foresters families whose livelihoods and well-being depended on it. But David's remarkable Military career, which made him something of a legend in the British Army (he was after all one of only two British officers to be awarded three Military Crosses during the War), was just a prelude to a lifetime of remarkable public service. Initially serving on Radnorshire County Council after returning home from the Army, he fought two close General Elections in his home constituency of Brecon & Radnor before becoming the Conservative Member of Parliament for Hereford at a by-election in 1956 (defeating Robin Day no less who was the Liberal candidate).

56

Quickly making his mark at Westminster, including a spell as Shadow Secretary of State for Wales, he eventually became a Welsh Office Minister in the Heath Government of 1970- 74. A Civil Servant who observed his first meet-the-staff tour of the Welsh Office Building in Cathays Park, Cardiff, reported that as he went around the building numerous members of staff stood stiffly to attention, such was the respect with which he was held and the reputation that went before him. In addition, he was blessed with impeccable manners and taste, striking good looks and an imposing height of 6'6", which his military bearing accentuated. Indeed, his friend the late Lord Geraint of Ponterwyd, whose time as Liberal MP for Ceredigion and North Pembrokeshire coincided with David's time in Parliament, described him as 'the best-looking man in the House of Commons'. If that was not enough, Nature had also bestowed on him great sporting prowess – an accomplished shot and a fine cricketer, once scoring a century in the annual Commons v Lords cricket match. David's decades of public life involved him in a great many roles outside the field of party politics.

One of his proudest achievements was, as Chairman of the British Livestock Export Council, arranging the first British Agricultural Exhibition in the Soviet Union in Moscow in 1964, at the height of the Cold War. One can only imagine the difficulties that such a project entailed, but it was a great success, securing many orders from Russian collective farms. It also included a meeting on at least one occasion for him and his wife Diana, with the Soviet Leader Kruschev. That success reflected David's passion for matters rural. His estate in the rugged upper Wye Valley included a herd of pedigree Welsh Black cattle, which Diana initially did much to develop and expand, the work later continued by their son Robin to the point where the herd was renowned across Wales and the UK. Half the estate was and is native and commercial forests and David was an expert forester.

Post his retirement from active politics in 1974, he served as Wales Forestry Commissioner for 10 years; was Chairman of Timber Growers, UK 1989- 1990, and its President from 1993- 1998. His maiden speech in the House of Lords, upon his ennoblement in 1979, as in the House of Commons almost thirty years earlier, was on the subject of forestry. David's commitment to rural Wales was rewarded when he was made President of the Royal Welsh Agricultural Society Show in 1976 and he was Chairman of the Society's Council from 1977 to 1994, playing a leading role in expanding the Show into Europe's largest such event. Somehow, he found time to be a member of the Historic Buildings Council Wales from 1975-1979 and to chair the winning 'No Assembly' campaign in the 1979 devolution referendum. Lord Hailsham as Lord Chancellor appointed him Chairman of the Council on Tribunals, an important part of England & Wales justice system, from 1980 to 1986.

So, David Gibson-Watt was an outstanding example of British military and public service, the like of which we see much less of nowadays, driven not by ambition or personal gain but by the notion of duty, exemplified by the fact that, despite his extensive wider commitments, he continued to serve as a local Magistrate in Rhayader for many years until his retirement at the age of 70. He gained the reputation of being "the most honest and decent man in politics".

It would be foolish and naïve to suggest that these levels of commitment over so many decades did not place strains on his wife Diana (nee Hambro, a daughter of Sir Charles Hambro, the well-known City financier and Head of SOE during the Second World War) and their family of two boys and two girls. Their eldest child Jamie had died very young in 1946 of leukaemia, a source of lifelong sorrow for them both. It is perhaps telling that, although his and Diana's deep love and marriage endured until death, none of their children followed David into elected office at any level, indicative perhaps of the toll that the public service provided by people like David Gibson-Watt, from which we mere mortals benefit so mightily, inevitably comes at some cost to those they love the most.

One of the things that kept David Gibson-Watt going through all his ups and downs was a fundamental belief in Christianity, which gave the foundation to his work and behaviour.

ENOCH POWELL

Enoch Powell is best known for his notorious 'Rivers of Blood' speech in 1968 and his outspoken opposition to immigration.

He was one of the most controversial figures in British political life in the second half of the 20th century and a formative influence in what came to be known as 'Thatcherism'.

Enoch Powell

Powell was born into early 20th century Birmingham. The Powells originated in Radnorshire, the Welsh Border county but migrated into the industrial West Midlands coalfields. He always seemed to retain an interest in Wales and in October 1948 was working for the Secretariat and Research department of the Conservative Party. His approach to Wales was very sensitive and he insisted that social and political factors should not be subordinated to Laissez Faire economics. He formulated an eleven page paper to ascertain what the general direction should be for Conservative policy in rural Wales. Among his suggestions he favoured steps to demonstrate the party's sympathy with the Welsh language including Welsh speaking candidates in Welsh speaking areas. He also said there was a need with the for some single authority in or with access to the Cabinet and charged with ensuring attention to Welsh interests in all spheres of government.

Powell's reports formed the basis of Conservative policy in Wales. Rab Butler drew heavily on Powell's recommendations for the statement of policy for Wales and Monmouthshire, the so called Welsh Charter which was finally launched on St David's Day 1st March 1949. It was Powell who suggested the charter was published in both English and Welsh.

As a Tory representing an English seat, Powell's regular intervention in Welsh business in the Commons irritated the large contingent of Labour MPs from the Principality. He attended a special meeting of Welsh Tories in Ludlow in late May 1951. Powell was concerned with defining the responsibilities and status of the proposed Minister for Welsh Affairs. He was a great one for debunking the arguments for devolution but felt the Welsh should be recognised in government. It is pertinent that Powell, who was very interested in languages should have developed an interest in Medieval Welsh, an interest which he pursued for many years. He discovered a Welsh Medieval text that intrigued him, a task that led him unaided to develop his rudimentary knowledge of Welsh into a good understanding of Medieval Welsh. He wrote a paper on the text for the Bulletin of the Board of Celtic Studies. His work excited the interest of the Welsh scholar Stephen Williams of Swansea University who contacted Powell but their collaboration was interrupted by Powells going abroad and the coming of war. But finally in 1942 they published Llyfr Blegywryd as a study of the laws of the Welsh King Howell the Good.

In October 1941, Powell was posted to Cairo as a member of the Royal Warwickshire Regiment. He became Secretary to the Joint Intelligence Committee Middle East. In August 1942 he was promoted to Lt Colonel and helped plan the 2nd Battle of Alamein. His job was unrelenting in the number of hours he worked and it was at this time he became very suspicious of the United States and its policy towards the British Empire. After the victory of El Alamein, he secured a posting to the British Imperial Army in Delhi as a Lt Colonel in Military Intelligence. He was appointed secretary to the Joint Intelligence Committee for India and tried to get assigned to the Chindits, but unfortunately did not succeed as especially Orde Wingate had taken a great dislike to Powell. Looking back on his military career, Powell said one of his greatest moments was when he was promoted from private to lance corporal, describing it as a greater promotion than entering the Cabinet. After that he rose rapidly up the ranks, eventually becoming a brigadier.

He always remained firm in his belief that the United Kingdom should be a single nation. He eventually went over to Ireland, to Ulster as an MP and took on the concern that Ulster should remain an incontrovertible part of the Union. Powell had many of the characteristics of a Welshman and had much to say about Wales in his career but was fundamentally against devolution.

LORD CHALFONT

Lord Chalfont died a month after reaching his 100th birthday on 10th January 2020. He was a regular soldier with the South Wales Borderers who, soon after he finished wearing uniform was in October 1964 plucked from the world of journalism to become a minister in Harold Wilson's first Labour government. Colonel Alan Gwynne Jones as he was known then was defence correspondent for the Times and was offered the post in the Foreign Office as the Minister for Disarmament.

He was born at Llantarnam and educated at West Monmouthshire School. He joined the 6th SWB in 1940. He saw nearly 3 years of action in Burma, where he finally commanded A Company of the battalion. He was a great rugby player, and after the end of World War 11 he moved into military intelligence. After a time in staff college he was posted back to regimental duty to command B Company. On 1st December 1965 he directed a dangerous patrol that led to the killing of 2 of the notorious Selumpur branch of the terrorists. He personally shot the leader and led the charge that overtook and killed the second in command. Wounded, the terrorists ran with the grenade towards his hiding place, disregarding a hail of bullets. Major Gwynne Jones shot the terrorist and seized and disabled the grenade which he was carrying before it could go off. This action caused Gwynne Jones to be recommended for a Military Cross for his eagerness to take on any operation, no matter how dangerous with remarkable stamina and personal gallantry. He returned from Malaya in spring 1958 and was posted to Cyprus to command B Company 1RWF for operations against EOKA terrorists. He was keen to command 1SWB but there was too much competition for it. He joined The Times as defence correspondent and he only left it to become a member of the government.

After the General Election in 1970 which brought Conservative Prime Minister Edward Heath to power, Lord Chalfont became a front bench opposition spokesman until he resigned from the Labour Party in 1972 when the Labour party made a u turn and decided not to pursue the policy of joining the EEC. He subsequently became a cross bencher in the Lords and held a number of public and business board appointments. As chairman of Vickers Ship Building, he oversaw the construction of Britain's Trident Submarine Fleet. Between 1980 and 1984 he chaired the Lords All Party Defence Group. He retired as an active member of the House of Lords in 2015. He published a number of books including his autobiography. There is no doubt he was a brave man.

NYE BEVAN AND JENNIE LEE

By The Rt Hon Nick Thomas-Symonds MP

(Shadow Secretary of State for International trade)

In 1949, Time magazine featured Nye Bevan on its front cover, reporting that he had stood "amid the tall black blocks of Bolton's cotton mills in Lancashire and told the assembled workers: "homes, health, education and social services – these are your birth- right." " This was an indication of the scale of the change in society Bevan had brought about in creating the National Health Service that had come into existence in July the previous year. As Minster of Health and Housing in Clement Attlees post- war Labour Government from 1945 to 1951, the impact of what Bevan achieved was to make access to healthcare a right people came to expect, not a luxury commodity that was only available to those who could afford it. The son of a miner, Bevan was born in Tredegar in 1897, and started work down the pit himself at the age of 13 in 1911.

Nye Bevan

As he grew up, Bevan drew a profound conclusion: that poverty was not the fault of individuals, as the Victorian attitude would have it; rather, it was caused by Conservative Governments that failed to properly mobilise the resources of the country and distribute them more equally. This was captured in his sarcastic remark that "This island is almost made of coal and surrounded by fish. Only an organising genius could produce a shortage of coal and fish in Great Britain at the same time."

He was determined to change this, and his mind turned to how: "A young miner in a South Wales Colliery, my concern was with the one practical question: Where does power lie in this particular state of Great Britain, and how can it be attained by the workers?" Ahead lay his route into Parliament to exercise the power to make a difference. Bevan drew lessons from his local community. The Tredegar Medical Aid Society, founded in 1890, which was a model for the National Health Service. Members paid a contribution in order to access healthcare free at the point of delivery. Bevan took this idea of people coming together to provide healthcare based upon need, and built upon it, as he ensured that the National Health Service was funded from general taxation rather personal subscription.

His experience in local government was also formative, as he served on both the Tredegar Urban District Council and Monmouth's County Council. He saw the vulnerability of local government budgets to central government spending cuts, leading him to ensure that the hospitals were nationalised under the National Health Service Act of 1946, rather than be run by local authorities. Under his system, the Government of the day would have responsibility for funding the National Health Service, rather than being able to cut it's resources and blame local Councils.

Bevans experience as a local Councillor also influenced his approach to the housing aspect of his Cabinet role. He knew the damage to public health that was caused by mass- built, poor quality housing. In his mind was the collier returning from a long shift, going straight into the bath on their return home. They should not have to clean themselves in a tin bath in the living area; instead, there should be a separate bathroom. Cramped housing affected quality of life. As he put it: "A rabbit warren house leads to a rabbit warren mind." Despite a timber shortage, and the need to divert labour away from constructing homes to producing products for export to deal with the balance of payments, by 1950 the Labour Government was building over 200,000 houses a year. Bevan's stirring oratory, his grasp of detail, and firm strategic direction made him a formidable Cabinet Minister.

He was a great statesman whose comprehensive healthcare system has benefited generations of people. In Danny Boyle's moving opening ceremony to the 2012 Olympic Games in London, the National Health Service was featured as a remarkable British achievement. Throughout the coronavirus pandemic, the National Health Service, with its magnificent staff, provided the universal healthcare provision Bevan imagined it always would in the months he spent establishing it.

The time Bevan spent in government did, however, come at a great personal cost. He was incredibly busy, and under immense strain. First, there were painstaking negotiations with the British Medical Association, to persuade the doctors to co-operate with the new health service. Then, there was the battle in Cabinet against charges being introduced for teeth and spectacles in 1951, which the Chancellor, Hugh Gaitskell, argued, was necessitated by a vastly-increased defence programme to which the Government had committed itself under American pressure after the outbreak of the Korean War. Bevan was, initially, moved to the Ministry of Labour, before resigning from the Government altogether in April 1951. This, in turn, contributed to significant pressure on his wife Jennie Lee. As she put it, there were "moments of intolerable strain when I felt I was being suffocated, when I almost went under."

Lee and Bevan shared a Celtic mining heritage: she was the daughter of a collier, born in 1904 on the Fifeshire coalfield. Highly intelligent, Lee was educated at Edinburgh University. Like Bevan, she was a fine public speaker, and was first elected to Parliament in 1929 for North Lanarkshire. She had her first serious conversation with Bevan, elected that same year for Ebbw Vale, on the House of Commons terrace, and was appalled by his suit, that she thought was a combination of Nonconformist Welsh Minister and ambitious stockbroker; actually, Bevan's mother Phoebe had bought it from the Tredegar Co-operative! Lee lost her seat in the catastrophic Labour General Election defeat of 1931, but her relationship with Bevan continued to develop. He proposed to her over dinner at the Café Royal in May 1934, and they were married at the Holborn Registry Office that October.

Jennie Lee

The advancement of Bevan's political career undoubtedly held Lee back. When she returned to the House of Commons in 1945, having won the seat of Cannock Chase, she was less assertive, as she recalled: "I did not speak with the same fluency as I had done in the 1929- 31 Parliament. Any time Nye had a difficult speech to make, I would be in the Chamber, half looking forward to it, half apprehensive. It was always a relief when it was safely over." When Bevan sought election to Labours National Executive Committee, Lee held back: "If I had stood...and been elected, that would have meant one place less for other friends whose support Nye needed." With Labour losing power in 1951, Lee seemed, for the time being, to have sacrificed her own chance to make her mark as a government minister. In the event, it was after Bevans death from stomach cancer in July 1960 that Lee's own political career flourished. When Labour returned to power in 1964, the new Prime Minister, Harold Wilson, appointed Lee as Minister of the Arts. As Leader of the Opposition, speaking in Glasgow in September 1963, Wilson had promised to create a "University of the Air". Those who left school at sixteen to work could still, later in life, study for a degree; those with regrets about not continuing in formal education could have a second chance; and others trained in one area could acquire new skills. Nobody, regardless of age or experience, would be excluded from the opportunity to make the most of their potential.

It was an inspiring vision, and Lee's job was to make it a reality. This she did, working with Wilson to ensure that the idea of the Open University was never dropped as a consequence of the various rounds of spending cuts that the Government had to deal with between 1964 and 1970. So committed to the project was Lee that, on 18 May 1970, when Wilson called a General Election for 18 June, and she was at Walton Hall with Lord Mountbatten laying the foundation-stone for the Open University, her immediate reaction was to protect it. As the news came through on the radio, her first action was the call her senior civil servant, Ralph Toomey, to tell him: "For God's sake, get out the letter giving the OU its grant."

The Open University was to endure, despite Labour losing the election. As millions of people have benefited from Bevan's greatest achievement, the National Health Services, over two million students have also enrolled in the Open University that has made lifelong learning a reality for generations of people. That edition of Time magazine from 1949 featured a lone Bevan; it would have been fitting, had a further edition been produced before Lees death in 1988, that she was on the front cover alongside him.

Time, 21 March 1949. Labour Party, Report of the 44th Annual Conference (London: Labour Party, 1945), p.132. Aneurin Bevan, *"In Place of Fear"* (London: Quarter Books edition, 1978), p.21. Merthyr Express, 5 September 1925.

For an account of Bevan's record on house- building, see Nicklaus Thomas- Symonds, *"The Political Life of Aneurin Bevan"* (London: I.B. Tauris, revised 2018 edition), pp.151- 161.

Jennie Lee, *"My Life With Nye"* (London: Jonathan Cape, 1980), p.195. p.197. Patricia Hollis, *"Jennie Lee: A Life"* (Oxford: Oxford University Press, 1997), p.338. https://www.open ac.uk/about/main/strategy and policies/facts and figures.

THE CONSERVATIVES in the 20th CENTURY

The Conservative Party has always been a little alien to Wales as, for a long time, it did not have many natural roots there. The Secretary of State, if he was a Conservative, was often seen as a viceroy. It was probably John Redwoods tenure in that position which gave the edge to a 'Yes ' referendum for the Assembly.

Lady Thatcher was probably the biggest Conservative, but she wrote to the author and said her family did not originate from Wales, but from Northamptonshire. However, John Campbell, her great biographer, in his book on her, said the Roberts side of her family came originally from Wales. It was very unusual for her not to know that this was the case although she might have found it inappropriate to mention her Welsh ancestry, especially after her battle with the Welsh miners. Having denied her Welsh ancestry, I thought it inappropriate to put her in the book.

It is interesting that Charles Powell was her foreign affairs advisor and that his brother Jonathan was Blair's chief of staff, perhaps another Welsh connection.

Another great man whose roots were in Wales, as he was a Cecil, was the 3rd Marquis of Salisbury 1830-1903. He served as Prime Minister 3 times over a period of 13 years. Historians have agreed that he was a strong and effective leader in Foreign Affairs with a wide grasp of the issues. He was a representative of the landed aristocracy and he held very reactionary views.

DAVID VIVIAN PENROSE LEWIS

First Baron Brecon 1905 - 1976

He was born on14th August 1905, the son of Alfred William and Elizabeth Mary Lewis of Craiglas, Talbont on Usk.

He was educated at Monmouth School to the age of 16 when he left to work with his father who owned stone quarries and slag merchants. He himself made a huge contribution to the development of quarrying and the Vaynor quarry became one of the largest and most advanced in Wales. As a youngster he showed interest in local politics and obtained a seat on Breconshire County Council in 1946. He was a big Conservative and was chair of the B&R Conservative Association 1947-51. He was made chairman of the Welsh Conservatives in 1956 and he was also a keen sportsman which is how the authors father got to know him well. He was President and Captain of the Crickhowell cricket team and a rugby player with both the Abergavenny team and the Crawshays 15 formed by his friend Geoffrey Crawshay. On 3rd December 1957 after much talk of a new element of devolution, the Cabinet agreed to support a Minister of State for Welsh Affairs, to which appointment Vivian Lewis was called and made Lord Brecon. However, there were objections in that his role was imprecise and that he lacked executive power.

He began as an energetic minister looking at the problems facing the state quarry industry, but also he was soon establishing the Development Corporation for Wales. The Corporation was an organisation of Welsh industrialists free from government control and finance. He did say that he did not speak Welsh but understood a certain amount. Lord Brecon served as Minister of State to Henry Brooke from 1957-61 and to Sir Keith Joseph from 1962-64. He was instrumental in the appointment of Sir Francis Jones as Wales Herald Extraordinary. He sold his company to

Powell Dyffryn in January 1964. From December 1972 to the summer 1973 he was nominated to the Conservative Delegation for the European Parliament where he raised questions on Welsh matters. He was chairman of the Welsh National Water Development Authority from 1973 to his death on 10th October 1976.

It was said he did not have a huge public persona but was more a grafter behind the scenes and served Wales in many roles. A likeable man, who maybe was not the most notable of Welsh politicians but was in at the beginning of devolution and therefore made his mark.

GEOFFREY HOWE

Margaret Thatchers deputy Prime Minister Geoffrey Howe was born in Port Talbot in 1926, joined Edward Heaths government as Solicitor General in 1970, and served in Margaret Thatcher's Cabinet as Chancellor of the Exchequer 1979–83, Foreign Secretary 1983-89 and Deputy Prime Minister 1989–90. He was made a Life Peer in 1992, with the title Lord Howe of Aberavon.

Geoffrey Howe

Even his wife Elspeth complained that he was a fiery Welshman, and the Howes were Welsh speakers and had lived in Glamorgan since at least the C17th. He went to prep school in Abberley Hall near Worcester, which gave him a chance to fulfil his father's ambition for him to go to a top school and Winchester was chosen. The 2 Howe boys first realised they spoke with a Welsh accent when the all England teasers got to work – in a few short weeks the Welshness had been all but washed away, although it sometimes crept back.

He did his National Service with the Royal Signals, where he did almost 2 years in Nanyuki at the foot of Mount Kenya. He went from the Signals to Trinity Hall, Cambridge, and he became chairman and vice chairman respectively of the college and university law societies. His failure to get a first in his final year was excused by his out of college activities, such as mountaineering in Snowdonia and the Alps, yachting on the Broads, and editing as much as writing for Oxford's Isis Magazine and he also experienced his first love.

When Mrs Thatcher came to power, he supported her economic policies and was a keen monetarist. He believed in balancing the books and keeping the money supply low to counter inflation. He became interested in Europe and was certainly for an accommodation with the EU, much more so than his leader.

His performance in the House of Commons was hardly charismatic. In fact, Dennis Healey said, 'A debate with Geoffrey Howe was like being savaged by a dead sheep.'

He resigned from the Thatcher government after much disagreement and his final speech was fairly devastating against her government. It was probably the knife in the back for Mrs Thatcher. He was a man of huge integrity and followed his conscience, which made him very wary of Thatchers approach to Europe. He was a fine Welshman with an outstanding brain and for a long time, a man of great loyalty to Mrs Thatcher and the Conservative Party.

MICHAEL HESELTINE

In Conservative circles, Michael Heseltine has been the victim of some snobbery about his background, 'the trouble with Michael is that he had to buy all his furniture'.

John Heseltine, his grandfather, with his wife and 4 children lived in a large house 'Brynteg' in a terraced road on Swansea's Mount Pleasant. His father Rupert had joined the army and in his late 20's he served for 5 years in the Royal Engineers and became an expert in bridge building. His father married Eileen Pridmore a 24 year old local woman. Her father had considerable means as a coal merchant.

Michael Heseltine

Michael Heseltine was born on 21st March 1923. His parents were sufficiently well off to employ two servants, a nurse and a cook. At the time, the family lived in a three-storey terraced house in Eaton Crescent in Uplands, less than ten minutes walk from the sea and about a mile from the centre of Swansea. Believe it or not, Michael was considered quite shy and 'only mischievous sometimes'. He once said, 'I am a Swansea boy. I come from the commercial middle classes of South Wales'. A local man once said, 'It was a very dug in middle class community, full of frightful snobs'. Most boys from the area were sent to public schools, usually across the border in England.

When the Second World War broke out, his father returned to the Royal Engineers where he held the rank of major. Michael was sent to a preparatory school at Llanwrtyd Wells which belonged to Bromsgrove School and had been evacuated to this small Welsh village. Michael was not terribly happy there and changed schools a couple of times and ended up in a prep school Broughton Hall. His father was a natural Conservative and in 1951 as Colonel Heseltine was appointed as deputy lieutenant for Glamorgan. Michael hero worshipped his father and generally, when they moved back to Swansea, he had plenty of interests and friends around Swansea and the Gower. After prep school, he was sent to Shrewsbury School, which stood alongside Eton, Harrow, Winchester, Westminster, Charterhouse and Rugby in the pecking order of public schools. Although he was undistinguished in the early years at school, he was certainly distinctive and people recall him as a bit of a loner. He was poor at sport and had little eye for the ball. He did however make the school athletics team as a high jumper.

He was quite lucky to be accepted by Pembroke College Oxford and he shone in student politics and debates, becoming president of the Oxford Union.

His choice of regiment for National Service was the Welsh Guards. He was not long there and was able to cut short his term of service by being a Parliamentary candidate.

Sir Charles Guthrie who became chief of the Defence Staff and served with him said, 'His contemporaries liked him and enjoyed his company, but I do think some of the more senior officers in the battalion were irritated by the fact that he made it fairly plain that he would prefer to be doing something other than soldiering'. He trained as an accountant and eventually managed to build a nearly £150 million fortune almost from nothing. He married Anne Williams and she was originally from a Welsh background and had studied languages at University College London.

He moved from the Tavistock constituency to the Henley one and outside that constituency he bought a large country house. He held a number of positions in the Thatcher government, but his views diverged a lot from her 'tooth and claw' capitalism. He finally fell out with her over the Westland affair and resigned from the cabinet. Then he gradually got together enough support to take her on in a leadership contest. He did so well that she was driven to stand down, although he was not able to win the contest. He is a great longstanding supporter of Europe, and his opposition to 'Brexit' has been colourful and rigorous.

MICHAEL HOWARD

His family were originally a Jewish family from a remote part of Eastern Europe. They came to Llanelli as immigrants. Barely a year after Bernat and Hilda had married, on 7th July 1941 they had a baby who was called simply Michael. Bernat Hecht applied for citizenship and changed their name to Howard. 'I knew he was going somewhere from the very beginning,' says Jean Pugh who taught Michael Howard at primary school.

Michael Howard

'He was an extremely nice chap, exceptionally pleasant, quiet, unassuming and polite.' It was quite a big school, a few hundred yards up the hill from the family home. Harriet Griffiths, who taught Michael at ages nine and ten, says he was a very diligent scholar. He also acquired a Welsh accent. The Howards ate Kosher food at home, and regularly attended the local synagogue, but although they regarded themselves as fully orthodox Jews, they were not always fully observant.

In 1952 Michael took the 11 plus exam and entered Llanelli Grammar School, which was all boys. The school was clean, disciplined and orderly, and consisted of 600 boys. Most of the boys were sons of miners, tin plate workers or people in the steel plate industry. Perhaps 2 per cent of the parents owned their own businesses. He was cleverer than most pupils and he had asthma which meant he always missed games, which was a disadvantage in an all boys school. Michael took more interest in soccer than he did rugby.

He was a formidable debater in school, and he joined the Jewish Youth Group in Swansea and during the Christmas and summer holidays he went on camps organised by the Jewish Youth Study Group. To start with, some of his teachers were reluctant to see him apply for Cambridge, and he didn't get far with a number of Cambridge colleges until Peterhouse accepted him to read economics.

His passions in life were for The Beatles, American Baseball and Liverpool. It took him almost twenty years to secure a safe seat in Parliament and then he went on to be a minister. He was behind the poll tax, section 28, and the idea that prison works, but also, as Home Secretary he presided over a substantial drop in crime. He came back to lead his party, but only to a third resounding defeat. He wooed one of the most beautiful women of his generation, who is now one of his greatest assets, Sandra Paul, the international model, who was holidaying with Frank Sinatra and dining with JF Kennedy while her future husband was still a student. He had come a long way since his roots in Llanelli.

TRISTAN GAREL-JONES

Born in Gorseinon, Wales, the son of Bernard Garel-Jones and Meriel nee Williams, he and his family moved first to Las Palmas in the Canary Islands, prior to settling in Madrid, Spain when he was 7 years old. He was educated at King's School, Canterbury, while his parents established successful language schools in Spain and he then moved back to the United Kingdom and worked as a merchant banker prior to moving to a career in politics.

The author met him when the former won a prize to have tea in the House of Commons. Garel-Jones interest was sparked when he discovered his grandfather had worked in the author's great grandfather's coal mine. He first contested Caernarvon in 1974 but was defeated by the future leader of Plaid Cymru, Dafydd Wigley. When it came to the leadership contest, he voted for Margaret Thatcher in the first round, but if it went to a second round, he would vote for Douglas Hurd. His house was used as the plotting ground against Thatcher, and he himself was seen as a mixture of Machiavelli and Ivan the Terrible by the Thatcherite right wing.

He is said to have been the inspiration for the fictional scheming Whip Francis Urquhart in the novel, 'House of Cards. He was a very effective Whip and delivered many votes in favour of Thatcher's legislation. He could be described as 'Another scheming Welshman'.

WILLIAM HAGUE

Hague was born on 26th March 1961 in Rotherham Yorkshire. He initially boarded at Ripon Grammar School and then attended Wath Comprehensive School. His parents Nigel and Stella Hague ran a soft drinks manufacturing business where he worked during the school holidays. He first made the national news at the age of 16 by addressing the Conservatives at their annual National Conference in 1977. He read Philosophy, Politics and Economics at Magdalen College Oxford. He was President of the Oxford University Conservative Association and President of the Oxford Union. At a by-election in 1989 he was elected as a member for the safe Conservative seat of Richmond.

He was invited to join the Government in 1990 serving as Parliamentary Private Secretary to the Chancellor of the Exchequer. In 1995 he was made Secretary of State for Wales, succeeding John Redwood who had been heavily criticised for being seen on television apparently miming the National Anthem at a conference. Hague sought a Welsh Office civil servant Ffion Jenkins to teach him the words. They were later married.

Following the 1997 General Election defeat of the Conservatives he was elected as Leader of the Conservative Party in succession to John Major. His authority was challenged by the appointment of Michael Portillo as Shadow Chancellor, although the latter lost his seat at the 1997 General Election. In 2015 Hague purchased a £2.5 million country house Cyfronwydd, outside Welshpool in Powys.

After David Cameron was elected leader in 2005, he went on to become Camerons deputy and was appointed First Secretary of State and Foreign Secretary in 2010. He did not stand for re-election in 2015 and became a Life Peer. Since his retirement from public life, he has maintained a weekly column in the Daily Telegraph and had written books such as 'William Pitt the Younger', and 'William Wilberforce'. He is still writing and remains influential in the Conservative Party. Like Gladstone, he lives in Wales and has married a Welsh wife. He was generally considered sympathetic to Wales in his time as Secretary of State.

NICHOLAS EDWARDS, LORD CRICKHOWELL

Edwards was of Welsh stock, but he was born in London. His father was head of the furniture and woodwork department at the V&A Museum. The family had a home in the Black Mountains in South Wales, as well as one in Chiswick, West London. He was educated at Westminster School before going to Trinity College Cambridge to study history after National Service in the Royal Welch Fusiliers. After university he went into insurance in the City and in due course became a Lloyds broker. He was elected as Tory MP for Pembrokeshire at Edward Heath's triumphant General Election. It was a constituency that had supported Labour for 20 years and he would hold his seat throughout his Commons career. He was Welsh Secretary for 8 years during Margaret Thatcher's first two administrations.

He was a huge supporter of the Cardiff Bay development, despite its massive overshooting of cost. Although his credentials were economically dry, he was pragmatic in Wales and when Wales sole Plaid Cymru MP Gwynfor Evans threatened to starve himself to death to secure a separate Welsh language television service Edwards conceded that. Edwards realised and persuaded Margaret Thatcher that if Gwynfor Evans died, she would have another Ireland on her hands. So, sensibly, both backed away. He was equally vehement that the government should not be seen as philistine by cutting arts funding to the National Museum of Wales. He was keen on a new opera house for Wales and wanted a home for the Welsh National Opera in Cardiff. He was extremely keen on the arts. When, partly due to ill health he retired from the Commons he was the first chairman of the newly established National Rivers Authority and championed with great energy the improvement of water quality and the shaming, if necessary, and prosecution of industrial polluters. He was himself a freshwater angler and lived in a converted mill in the Black Mountains. He died on 17th March 2018.

Although initially seen as a Right Wing figure he adapted himself to a more Left Wing Wales and it was largely due to him and Sir Geoffrey Inkin that the Cardiff Bay project was completed successfully.

SIR ROBERT BUCKLAND QC

He was born on 22nd September in 1968 in Llanelli and was educated at the private school St Michaels in the town. He studied at Hatfield College, University of Durham and graduated in law in 1990 and the following year was called to the bar at the Inner Temple. He practised as a barrister in Wales from 1992 to 2010 and was appointed as a recorder in 2009, sitting as a part-time judge in the Crown Court. He was appointed Queen's Counsel in 2014 on becoming Solicitor General. He stood unsuccessfully for the Conservative Party as their candidate for Preseli, Pembrokeshire at the 1997 General Election. He was selected as the Conservative candidate for South Swindon which he won in the 2010 General Election. Also, in 2010 he was elected to the Justice Select Committee which promoted the successful banning of prisoners mobile phones in prisons. He became chair of the Conservative Human Rights Commission from 2011 to 2014. In July 2014 he was appointed Solicitor General for England and Wales and as Solicitor General, he took the Serious Crime Bill 2014 through the common stages in Bill committee.

This Bill contained provisions that updated the criminal law of child neglect and introduced a criminal offence of coercive control of people within close relationships.

In the 2015 General Election he retained his seat and in May 2019 he was appointed Minister of State for Prisons at the Ministry of Justice and in July 2019 he was appointed Justice Secretary and Lord Chancellor by Prime Minister Boris Johnson.

In December 2019 he was re-elected to his constituency and he was keen on increasing the number of prisons and also at the time,

he was against withdrawal from the EU, which possibly lost him some popularity with Boris Johnson. In 2011 he was awarded the Politician of the Year Award by the Royal College of Speech and Language Therapists, for his work on speech, language and communication issues. In January 2013 he was awarded the Grassroot Diplomat Initiative Award for his extensive work on advocating awareness at Parliament for children with special educational needs including those with autism.

He lives in Wroughton in Wiltshire and his interests include music, wine, political history and watching Rugby at cricket.

RAYMOND WILLIAMS,

A GREAT POLITICAL THINKER

It is fitting that in the first of these essays, we should celebrate the life of this great Welsh intellectual on the 100th anniversary of his birth. He was a socialist writer, academic, novelist and critic influential within the New Left. His writings on politics, culture, the media and literature contributed to the Marxist critique on culture and the arts.

Raymond Williams

Raymond Williams was born to Harry and Gwen Williams on the 31st August, 1921, in a rather ugly black stone house near the little villages of Pandy and Crucorney next door to the Offa's Dyke path. His father worked on the railways and had a shift on the signal box. His shifts were twelve hours at a time and 60 or 70 trains came through each day. Williams's novel 'Border Country' is centred on his father whom he described as "full of energy and driven to hard work." His mother Gwen Williams was stern and quiet and a hard task master with him. One of the themes that went through Raymond's life was the idea of community and its association with the Wales he grew up in. Although he lived most of his life in England, he saw himself as Welsh European and much of his writing was influenced by Marxism. His 1958 book 'Culture and Society' and the 1961 book 'The Long Revolution' were hailed as a testimonial to the theoretical, historical and critical development of English culture.

His main concentration was on his novels such as 'Border Country' and 'People of the Black Mountains'. He was on the board of a magazine 'The New Left Review' and he was always concerned with the social formation of class which seemed to lie at the centre of contemporary civilisation and was the cause of much discontent. His work and his background were based solidly on the Border Country. After a period at the Pandy Church of England Primary School he succeeded in getting into Abergavenny Grammar School. The great strength of Raymond Williams' kind of Socialism was that it was like the home-grown Socialism of William Morris and some of Raymond's views were coloured by Abergavenny's proximity to the Valleys and the coal mines and the huge battles that went on between the miners and the coal owners and later all the issues involved with class warfare. He was so successful at school that he was accepted by Trinity College, Cambridge, one of the great colleges where his Socialism was reinforced by his proximity to the privileged classes.

Before the war, while at Cambridge, much of his exertion went into the Socialist Club Bulletin. He was quite happy to join the officer training corps as a man convinced that he had to fight against Fascism. He left Cambridge to fight in the war and, after becoming engaged to Joy Dalling, described as a staunch, pretty, golden-haired woman and the anchor of his life, he started off at the Royal Signals Depot at Prestatyn. He was fit enough to fulfil the armys obsession with physical exercise and was soon designated as officer material. In January 1942 he was posted to officer cadet school at Larkhill. When asked to register his preference for regimental posting he put down anti-tank regiment first and he joined the 21st Anti-tank Regiment and camped on Salisbury Plain. Even to Williams the make up of the regiment had no clear class divisions in the officers' mess.

There was a good mixture including a garage owner, a Maltese refugee, two other students and an insurance agent. On 22nd June, 1944, at half past two in the afternoon, the regiment ran ashore on Juno Beach, D Day plus 16. On 28th June the regiment was deployed for action around the hamlet of Putot-Bessin. The fighting was heavy but quite sporadic. Raymond Williams became an acting captain. He said, 'How unlike the military history of battles it all was. There was always a dreadful sense of loss'. He was involved in the great battles around Caen. He felt the campaign was one, 'Where the men were swept along as in an unforeseeable tide and they were like mere flotsam'.

At a later stage of his life, he perceived the rawness of the Normandy experience could be seen in the wider social experience of the Spanish Civil War and the '84-'85 miners strike. Raymond carried with him always the unfulfilled duty to fallen comrades. He himself had shown undoubted bravery at Grainville-sur-Odon. His personal diary halts after the Normandy break and it picks up again on 6th September when the Grenadier Group which he was attached to reached Louvlein. After that the troops entered Brussels on 3rd September led by the Welsh Guards. 'Cheering crowds would not let us sleep until 0400 hours. They came back at 0700 hours and started all over again. The tanks by this time were completely covered with flowers.' Afterwards he was involved in Operation Market Garden and they took part in the Guards' armoured dash for Arnhem. The bridge at Nijmegen was taken. They failed to get to Arnhem in time and Q Battery in which Williams served was withdrawn in the second week of October for maintenance and rest.

Williams was not desperately impressed by many of the Guards officers around him whom he described as 'rather dull.' However, he had proved himself a capable and efficient officer and he was respected and liked by his troops. As regards his wider view of the war, he was always concerned with the suppression of liberated forces in Europe by British arms. He said, 'I only dread being personally involved in it as I would quite definitely face court martial rather than face serving in such circumstances'. Apart from certain vengeful

83

feelings against the Nazis, the power politics of the war's wake had made him too cynical to want or believe or to work for anything.

At the end of the war he was a very successful editor of the regimental newspaper, 'Twenty One'. He said, 'I have heard so many voices raised in mock horror at my suggestion that the memory of a Fascist soldier should be regarded in contempt and hate and never reverence.' He said, 'The banners of the Swastika that waved at Nuremberg carried death, lying, torture and famine to Guernica, Rotterdam, Rostoff and Coventry.' He went on, 'Three years before the war I was a Christian pacifist. The Sermon on the Mount was for me the final embodiment of the Truth. Faced with war, with Fascism, having seen what was happening to a Europe that was turning to Hitler its other cheek, I found it no longer satisfied me. I may have been wrong but the only people who attempt to translate the great principles of the Sermon on the Mount into political belief are the Christian pacifists. I respect them. The people I don't respect are the sitters on the fence who claim to accept Christian doctrine yet accepted and supported the war. If we were willing to kill, we are hypocrites or mercenaries; if we are not willing to hate let us go on hating Fascism which caused this destruction and go on working for all that is true, all that is noble, all that is human, all that is opposed to the horror we hated.'

He became, after the war, a famous and well-respected Cambridge don. His writing and lecturing had all the quality of Welsh Non Conformist Chapel. He saw Cambridge as an alien citadel which was to be overwhelmed by the ideas of Socialism. He was a man of his time who managed to accept the role of a successful officer attached to the Guards Armoured Division but, at the same time, preserved deeply his faith in Socialism and his aversion to the high citadels of embedded capitalism.

He was a Welshman through and through who encapsulated the Janus-like quality of the borders. He looked towards the English bastions of academic excellence for preferment although he was uncomfortable in them and critical of them; but it is probable that, if he had not been part of them, his voice would not have been heard

84

so widely. As a remarkable man of great intellect, he encapsulated the history of his time, his ideas generated debate all over the kingdom and, at the same time, he had showed his mettle and loyalty to freedom by his skill and courage as a British army officer.

His contribution to the debate in Wales has not been very well documented, but he was profoundly rooted in his native country, and his ideas of community and the divisions of Welsh society between the industrial areas and the country areas gave rise to much discussion among the Left Wing parties of Wales. Although his ideas were internationalist, he contributed much to the culture of Wales and especially its Left Wing parties. He was a widely respected commentator on the class struggle and was a great supporter of the miners. Although not a politician himself, he was full of political ideas and above all, he hated fascism.

'*Raymond Williams*' by Fred Inglis

'*Raymond Williams, a Warrior's Tale*' by Dai Smith

THE LABOUR PARTY IN THE 20TH CENTURY

After the Liberals faded, the Labour Party became the natural party of Wales and produced many fine politicians and even statesmen.

In a country ravaged by post industrialisation and with large swathes of poverty, they appealed to the majority of the voters especially those who felt themselves 'downtrodden'.

STEPHEN OWEN DAVIES 1886 – 1972

The Western Mail called him 'one of the most colourful, controversial and independent of the MPs elected from the Welsh mining valleys'. The South Wales Echo described him as 'A pacifist, a Socialist and a patriotic Welshman'. As a young man he was excluded from the Brecon Memorial College, a Congregationalist Foundation, for his radical religious beliefs and after being a combative miner's leader he was elected Labour MP for Merthyr Tydfil in 1934, a seat he held until his death.

He opposed what he regarded as Capitalist or Imperialist wars and those often appeared to give him an anti-west and pro-communist bias. He was often at loggerheads with the Labour government and boycotted the ceremony when Harold Wilson was made Freeman of the Borough of Merthyr Tydfil because of what he regarded as the government's cynical response to the Aberfan disaster. He was a lifelong supporter of Welsh self-government and proudly acted as one of Gwynfor Evans sponsors when he was introduced to the House of Commons after Plaid Cymru's historic win in the Carmarthen by-election of 1966.

He was deselected by his local party but stood as an independent

Socialist in the 1970 General Election and won by a mile, the only politician in living memory to beat the party machine. He was immediately expelled from the Labour Party and it is interesting in his last appearance in the House of Commons he voted against the Common Market.

JAMES GRIFFITHS

Ben Rees in his book on the life and work of James Griffiths emphasises the influences that shape the young Jim. These range from the Welsh patriotism embodied by poet brother Amanwy to the close-knit mining communities that characterise the Amman Valley. The religious revival of 1904 was a turning point for Jim who became committed to changing the world for the better. Then came the Independent Labour Party with Jim a founding member of the branch locally in 1908. He was a very effective political operator soon afterwards when he was instrumental as a political agent for the Labour Party holding Llanelli in 1923. He rose from miners agent in 1925 to the president of the FED in the mid 1930s.

When he went into Parliament he worked as Minister for National Insurance in Clement Attlees post war government. One of the crowns of his political career was the National Insurance and Industrial Injuries Act which gave enabling legislation for all sorts of casualties of the system. He championed the findings of the Beveridge Report during the Second World War. Serving as Colonial Secretary in the early 1950s he became an important figure for freedom movements globally. His skill at negotiation in some of the friction that existed between Wilson and Gaitskell was remarkable.

He wholeheartedly championed the Welsh language and culture. He loved Wales and always supported causes to promote Wales. He was vociferous in criticising the drowning of Capel Celyn. He was hugely enthusiastic for creating a Welsh Office with a Welsh Secretary of State where he came up against sceptics like Nye Bevan. He sat at the Cabinet table as the 1st Secretary of State in 1964. Two others of his priorities were to strengthen the legal status of the Welsh language and supporting the feasibility of setting up an elected Welsh Council. By the General Election of 1966 a distinctly Welsh Labour had become an unquestionable National Movement of Wales. They had won 32 out of the 36 constituencies. He left his Cabinet job and remained Llanelli's MP until 1970, 34 years after having been elected. His significance to Wales was elevating its status in Westminster and instilling our belief that we could govern relatively independently.

In many ways Jim was the architect of this revival.

MICHAEL FOOT

Michael Foot came from a well-known Devon family and was a left wing intellectual in the Labour Party. He was swept in after Nye Bevan in Ebbw Vale which Nye wanted him to stand in with 68% of the vote. He was hardly an ally of Gaitskells, disagreeing with him on foreign and defence policy. There was much argument between Gaitskell and the left wing.

Michael Foot

In Ebbw Vale he soon made friends aplenty. He became particularly friends with his agent and erstwhile challenger for the Labour nomination in the constituency, Ron Evans. A former steel worker, Ron seemed to Foot to embody almost all the South Wales virtues; his dedication to socialism and peace, his love of choral music, his rugby skills when he had played for the Ebbw Vale works in his younger days.

Jill, Foots wife also loved Ebbw Vale, her fascination with South Wales dating from her time making the film *Blue Star*. She spent much time in the constituency and was greatly liked there, taking part in various local activities although she was partly held to blame for Michael's shabby clothing. There were never any political problems in Ebbw Vale; Foot proceeded to win 8 successive General Election contests there between 1960 and 1982. His majorities were always upwards of 16,000 and he usually polled between 70-75% of the vote.

Michael and Jill made a home in Ebbw Vale. In 1961 they bought a house at 10 Morgan Street, one of a row of old iron workers houses. Foot went down to the constituency every weekend and held his surgeries in his Morgan Street home. It was generally agreed that he was a highly conscientious and hardworking constituency member and he worked considerably hard when the steel works got into difficulty in 1974 when he was a cabinet minister.

His first volume of the Life of Aneurin Bevan was published in 1962 and it was much welcomed.

Devolution was not an issue to which he had devoted much attention in his early career. His hero Bevan had been strongly centralist. Foot had enormous enthusiasm for the Welsh people, not only for their instinctive socialism and egalitarianism but also for their vibrant culture and enthusiasm for their language. Jill was even more pro Welsh than Michael They might both have reflected on Bevan's observation, 'The Welsh are good boy but they're not that good'. Foot took over the whole idea of devolution with all the zeal of a convert.

The 2nd reading of the devolution bill was passed comfortably on 17th December 1976, 10 Labour MPs voted against it. Cledwyn

Hughes wrote of Foot, ' He has made a greater effort to understand us and to meet Welsh aspirations than any other non Welsh politician I have ever known. He has stood up to cruel attacks which would have daunted lesser men. Foot has won an honourable place in Welsh history whatever may become of the bill.'

After this time, Foot was a huge supporter of the miners against Thatcher. In 1991 it was formally announced that Michael Foot would retire from Parliament in the next election.

JAMES CALLAGHAN

James Callaghans career has been unique. No other British politician has held the 4 great posts of Chancellor of the Exchequer, Home Secretary, Foreign Secretary and Prime Minister.

James Callaghan

In his early life, Callaghan knew poverty until, on leaving school he found employment and a measure of security with the Inland Revenue Service. With economic independence came independence

90

of mind.

He became a full time official of his trade union, embarked on a supremely happy marriage, served in the Royal Navy during the war, and entered politics in the heady year of 1945. He was encouraged to stand for Parliament and was adopted after defeating his chief rival George Thomas for the South Cardiff seat. One of the big issues was the nationalisation of the coal mines which was not seriously challenged by the Conservatives. He won a stunning victory based on the optimism promised by a future Labour government.

Callaghan was not a Welshman, but was an active trade unionist, having set up the Inland Revenue Staff Association. He was very involved in the Devolution bills and seemed to have few reservations about the concept of devolution. As Home Secretary he oversaw the deployment of United Kingdom soldiers in Northern Ireland. Although he had a flat in Cardiff, he didn't seem to spend much time there and ended up with a farm in Sussex. At one stage he was the longest serving MP and also the Father of the House. He was obviously dedicated to his Cardiff constituency but was very much a socialist rather than a Welshman, with no apparent roots in Wales. He wasn't a traditional left winger in the Labour Party and it was quite acceptable to him to eventually accept the title, 'Baron Callaghan of Cardiff'. It was very useful to his Cardiff constituency to have such an influential MP representing them.

TUDOR ELWYN WATKINS,

Baron Watkins of Glantawe 1903-1983

Tudor Watkins was born at Abercrave in the Swansea Valley on 9 May 1903, the son of County Councillor Howell Watkins JP a Baptist deacon and lay preacher. He received elementary education but put in a lot to extramural classes organised by the WEA although he left school at 13½ and became a coal miner from 1917-25. He became the Labour Party agent in Brecon and Radnor from 1928-33. He was a very popular Labour MP from the General Election of 1945 until

91

his retirement in 1970. he was known as a man who put his constituency before his party. He was pro devolution and became the PPS to the Right Hon James Griffiths the First Secretary of State for Wales. He was Chairman of the Parliamentary Select Committee on Agriculture 1966-68. After his retirement from Parliament, he spent much time serving local government. He was an alderman and chairman of the Breconshire County Council and also the first chairman of the new Powys County Council from 1974-77 and Lord Lt of Powys from 1975-78. He was chairman of the Brecon Beacons National Park Committee and also served as secretary of the Abercrave Athletic Club, Cricket Club and the Ystralyfera Football League.

Although he was a lifelong diabetic, he managed to overcome the problems associated with this illness. He is credited with preserving the only known population of the Lesser Whitebeam tree. which was endangered in 1947 by British Army mortar practice in and around it's habitat. He raised the issue in the Commons and induced the War Secretary to pull out of the area. He was an institution in Brecon and Radnor before the boundaries were changed to make it a far less Labour dependable area.

A great local politician.

LORD CLEDWYN

Cledwyn Hughes was born in Holyhead and was educated at Holyhead Grammar School and at the University of Wales Aberystwyth where he studied law and became president of the Liberal Society. Hughes qualified as a solicitor in 1940. During the 2nd World War he served in the RAF VR in an administrative role, achieving the rank of Lieutenant. Meanwhile he had become a member of the Labour Party. In the 1945 election he came close to beating Lady Megan Lloyd George in the vote for the Anglesey constituency.

In the 1951 General Election he ousted her by 595 votes. He

increased his majority in the 1955 election. He supported the Parliament for Wales campaign and he also supported efforts to secure a Secretary of State for Wales. In 1957 he went to St Helena on behalf of the Labour Party and wrote a critical report of the appalling poverty of the island's population.

When Labour came to power in 1964 he was appointed Minister of State for Commonwealth Relations. He was very successful and his negotiating skills were marvellous, notably in Cyprus, Malaysia and the Indian sub-continent. In 1966 he was made Secretary of State for Wales but his first months were difficult, for instance in July 1966 Gwynfor Evans won the Carmarthen by-election and there was an upsurge in Nationalist support. He was pro devolution, and his time at the Welsh Office was deeply affected by the tragedy at Aberfan where a colliery spoil heap engulfed a primary school, leaving 144 dead, the vast majority of them children. In the subsequent enquiry it was said that Lord Robens, the National Coal Board chairman had misled Hughes in claiming that all tips were regularly inspected.

Hughes did much for Wales, revamping the Welsh Office and bringing the Royal Mint to Llantrisant. In 1968 he was moved to become Minister of Agriculture. He was sorry to leave the Welsh Office, especially as he had done much of the preparatory work for the Investiture of the Prince of Wales scheduled for 1969.

At Agriculture he transferred powers over agriculture in Wales over to the Welsh Office. He kept his seat in the 1970 election, however in 1972 he was dismissed by Harold Wilson for voting in favour of entry into the Common Market. He was always a strong European.

In 1976 Wilson resigned suddenly and Hughes was instrumental in the selection of James Callaghan as leader. In March 1977 he was actively involved in the negotiations that led to the Lib Dem pact. In late 1978 he was once again despatched as an envoy to Rhodesia but made little headway in persuading Ian Smith to co-operate. He also failed to persuade Joshua Nkomo to give up the armed struggle.

Cledwyn Hughes was always a mover and a shaker on the political

93

scene. He was the party go between in the Lib Lab pact and James Callaghan relied on him prominently in the negotiations, In 1979 at the end of a lengthy and distinguished career in the House of Commons Hughes endured 2 bitter disappointments, the loss of Anglesey to the Tories and the failure of devolution for Wales. In the House of Lords he headed an important delegation to see Willie Whitelaw or Lord Whitelaw as he was known, to persuade him not to abandon a Welsh television channel. Hughes was especially concerned at Gwynfor Evans threat to go on hunger strike if the channel was not adopted.

In November 1982 he became Leader of the Opposition in the House of Lords. His greatest achievement of the '80s was orchestrating a concerted and sustained attack criticising the controversial legislation of Margaret Thatcher on the Poll Tax.

His other great contribution in the House of Lords in the '80s was to organise and lead key opposition debates on the controversial issues of the day. At this time the House of Lords was televised and he became something of a celebrity. Perhaps his finest moment was in the critical negotiations over the establishment of the new Welsh TV channel S4C, which persuaded the government into a u turn so avoiding all the possible violence that would have been associated with the Gwynfor Evans hunger strike. In the House of Lords, he found a proper place for his talents as a conciliator and his abilities to combine the energies of people and groups across the political spectrum. He did much to water down some other more extremes of Thatcherism. He was essentially a man of the centre left.

LORD ELWYN JONES

Like another of our Lord Chancellors, Robert Buckland, he was born in Llanelli and read history at Gonville and Caius College Cambridge. He spent some time in Germany in the 1930s and was an acting bombardier in the Royal Artillery. He was commissioned as a second lieutenant on 23rd September 1939 and ended his service as a major. He became a barrister and recorder of Merthyr Tydfil and served as junior British Counsel during the Nuremburg Trials and led for the prosecution at the Hamburg Trial of Marshall Erich Von Manstein.

In 1966 he led the prosecution of the Moors murderers Ian Brady and Myra Hindley. At the 1950 General Election he became MP for West Ham South, serving until 1974. In 1964 he was appointed Attorney General and he served as Lord Chancellor from 1974 to 1979 and in 1976 he was made a Companion of Honour. His brother Idris was captain of the Wales rugby union team in 1925.

Lord Elwyn Jones died in December 1989 aged 80.

GEORGE THOMAS

Few politicians have won as much popular acclaim and affection as the Labour MP George Thomas, who became Speaker of the House of Commons and was later known as Lord Tonypandy. Towards the end of his life, he was something of a celebrity figure, spending his time on children's charities and socialising with Royalty and the great and the good. This view was summed up by his friend Margaret Thatcher, who described him as, 'A deeply committed Christian with a shining integrity'.

Throughout his life he was sustained by his Methodism. Thomas was born in Port Talbot, Glamorgan, the second son of Zachariah Thomas, a Welsh speaking miner from Carmarthen and Emma Jane Tilbury, daughter of a founder of the English Methodist Church in Tonypandy. His father became a heavy drinker and the family were happy when Zachariah joined up at the start of the 1st World War. He never returned to South Wales and died of tuberculosis in 1925.

George attended Trealaw Boys School where he passed the scholarship exam for Tonypandy Higher Grades School. On leaving he became a pupil teacher and attended a 2 year teacher training course at University College Southampton. He then worked as a teacher both in London and Cardiff. He stood for Parliament in 1945 and held Cardiff Central between 1945–50 and Cardiff West from 1950 until his retirement from the Commons at the 1983 General

Election. In April 1966 he was appointed Minister of State for Wales and was one of the first on the scene of the Aberfan Disaster in October 1966. He showed much sympathy to the people at first; the disaster cost the lives of 144 people, 116 of them children at Pantglas Junior School. The villagers campaigned vigorously for the remaining coal tips to be removed. In a meeting, Thomas refused to agree to their removal and the angry crowd took over the meeting while Thomas fled into hiding. However, he came back later and said the tips would be removed. He was involved in a decision by the government to forcibly take £150,000 from the Aberfan Charity Fund raised to help the victims as part payment for the removal operation. Only later, in 1997, 30 years after the disaster was the money paid back by Secretary of State Ron Davies.

Thomas was appointed Secretary of State for Wales from 1968–1970 and presided over the Prince of Wales' Investiture at Caernarvon Castle in 1969. He loved the Royal Family but had a barely disguised antipathy to his predecessor as Secretary of State for Wales Cledwyn Hughes whom he saw as a traitor for trying to promote limited devolution. He maintained an implacable opposition to nationalism, equally determined opposition to language pressure groups, and a major miscalculation in deciding that part of the cost of removing the coal tip at Aberfan should be taken from the money donated to the bereaved families. He also disliked Plaid Cymru, especially the Welsh Language Society. In 1976 he became Speaker of the House of Commons at the time of the first broadcasting of Parliamentary proceedings, which brought him to the attention of the public.

In July 1983 he retired and was raised to the Peerage with a hereditary Peerage as Viscount Tonypandy of Rhondda. He disliked the European Union and the Blair Government's Devolution proposals of 1997. He went on to endorse Sir James Goldsmith's Referendum Party. After Lord Tonypandys death, former Labour MP Leo Abse revealed in his book on Tony Blair, 'The Man Behind the Smile' that Thomas had been homosexual. Abse said he revealed this because Thomas's sexual orientation brought a feminine sensibility and empathy to politics. He also said that Thomas was a superb speaker in the House of Commons, was no saint, nor did he claim to be one. He claimed that the need to conceal his sexuality throughout his life because of punitive legislation and intolerant social attitudes meant that he was engaged in a continual battle with his own unworthiness. Throughout his career Thomas remained a deeply religious man and was a prominent member of the Methodist Church. He died in Cardiff on 22nd September 1997. He was twice engaged to be married but remained single.

PAUL MURPHY

(Baron Murphy of Torfaen)

His father Ronald was a miner of Irish descent. The family was devoutly Catholic; his mother Margery was English and her family were business people. He attended St Francis Roman Catholic School, Abersychan and West Monmouth School, Pontypool. He later attended Oriel College Oxford to study history. He was fascinated by the whole Oxford experience and loved his exposure to the arts and in particular music. He went on to be a lecturer in government and history at Ebbw Vale College of Further Education. This is where the author, who was desperately trying to achieve a 5th 'A' Level to get army sponsorship for university was taught by him and who succeeded in getting him an 'A' at 'A' Level. He was a tremendous teacher and he and the author remain friends to this day.

He has never married, and once said in an interview, 'I have so many books there is only enough room for me'. He joined the Labour Party at 15 and is a member of the Transport and General Workers Union. He was a member of Torfaen Council from 1973–87. He contested Wells Constituency in Somerset unsuccessfully in the 1979 election. He was MP for Torfaen from the 1987 Election; in opposition he served as a Foreign Affairs spokesman and then in defence as a Naval spokesman. He joined the Cabinet in July 1999 following his appointment as Secretary of State for Wales. In 2002 he moved departments and became Secretary of State for Northern

97

Ireland in which he served until his dismissal in the reshuffle which followed the 2005 Election.

Prior to joining the Cabinet, he was Minister of State for Political Development in the Northern Ireland office from 1997–99 acting as Mo Mowlans deputy. This was probably his finest hour as he was largely responsible for negotiating the so-called Strand 2 arrangements agreed in the Good Friday Agreement. He was absolutely crucial to these negotiations which became one of the Labour government's great successes. In 2013 he wrote a report on the lack of success of applicants to Oxbridge Universities from Welsh state schools. Ever since, he has campaigned for a set of regional hubs to link these hubs to top universities. Although he was a fierce opponent of Devolution, in 1997 he voted for it. In a free Parliamentary vote on 20th May 2008 Murphy voted for cutting the upper limit for abortions from 24 to 12 weeks. In 2013 he became one of the few Labour MPs to vote against the bill to legalise same sex marriages in England and Wales. He was probably one of the MPs admired most for his integrity. A man of great intelligence, moderation, and faith.

THE KINNOCKS

Neil Kinnock was an only child, and was born in Tredegar, Wales. His father was a former coal miner whose family originated in Scotland. His mother was a district nurse. He began his secondary education at Lewis School Pengam and went on to study at Cardiff University where he graduated in 1965 with a degree in industrial relations and history. The following year he obtained a postgraduate diploma in education. He has been married to Glenys Kinnock since 1967.

He was first elected to the House of Commons on 18th June 1970 and became a member of the National Executive Committee of the Labour Party in October 1978. Following Labour's defeat in the 1979 election, James Callaghan appointed Kinnock to the Shadow Cabinet as education spokesman. In the late 1980s Michael Foot replaced Callaghan as leader of the Labour Party. Kinnock was known as a left

winger and gained prominence for his attacks on Margaret Thatcher
and her handling of the Falklands War in 1982.

Neil Kinnock

When Michael Foot resigned, Kinnock was finally elected as
Labour Party leader on 2nd October 1983. His first period as Party
Leader between the 1983 and 1987 elections was dominated by
struggle with the hard left militant tendency.

The Labour Party was also threatened by the rise of the Social
Democrat Party/the Liberals. Kinnock focussed on modernising the
party and upgrading it's technical skills. He stressed economic growth

which had a much broader appeal to the middle class. The miners strike tested his loyalty to that group and in 2004 Kinnock said of Scargill, 'Oh, I detest him. I did then, I do now, and it's mutual. He hates me as well and I much prefer to have his savage hatred than even the merest hint of friendship from that man.'

In June 1986 the Labour Party finally expelled the deputy leader of Liverpool Council, a high profile militant supporter Derek Hatton. Peter Mandelson the Director of Communications had given the party a thorough rebranding. Labour now sported a continental style emblem of a rose. Michael Heseltine challenged Thatchers leadership and she resigned on 28th November 1990. She was succeeded by the then Chancellor of the Exchequer John Major.

In the 3 years leading up to the 1992 election Labour consistently topped the opinion polls. Labour's poll showing was pretty good at this time but Labours triumphalism in a Labour Party rally in Sheffield probably put many floating voters off. Kinnock later claimed he half expected his defeat in the 1992 election and proceeded to turn himself into a media personality. He announced his resignation as Party Leader on 13th April 1992.

He was an enthusiastic supporter of Ed Millibands campaign for leadership of the Labour Party in 2010. He became a European commissioner and was introduced to the House of Lords on 31st January 2005 although he was a long-time critic of the House of Lords and was accused of hypocrisy for joining it.

With regard to Welsh identity, he was one of just 6 MPs in South Wales who campaigned against devolution. He was also strongly opposed to 'Brexit'. He had married Glenys on 25th March 1967 and she was the UKs Minister for Africa and the United Nations from 2009 to 2010 and the Labour Member of the European Parliament from 1994 to 2009. She was made a life peer in 2009 and they have a son Stephen and daughter Rachel. Neil Kinnock, through his son Stephen is also the father in law of Helle Thorning Schmidt, the former Danish Prime Minister. Neil is a Cardiff City fan and also supports London Welsh RFC. He is said to be an agnostic and close to being an atheist.

BARON MORRIS OF ABERAVON

He was a Labour member of Parliament for over 41 years from 1959–2001, which included a period as Secretary of State for Wales from 1974-79. As of 2021 he is the only living former MP who was first elected in the 1950s. He is the last surviving member of Harold Wilson's 1974-79 cabinet and thereby the longest serving Privy Councillor. He was also made a Knight of the Garter. There seems to be some tradition that there is always a Welsh Knight of the Garter.

He was born in Capel Bangor near Aberystwyth and was educated at Ardwyn School, the University of Wales Aberystwyth and Gonville and Caius College Cambridge. He was a barrister and took Silk in 1973. Between 1982 and 1987 he was a recorder at the Crown Court. He was a man of great integrity and became Chancellor of the University of Glamorgan and was President of the Welsh Trust which runs the London Welsh Centre in Gray's Inn Road London. He was also a Council member of the Prince's Trust. Between 1997 and 1999 he returned to government as the attorney general for England and Wales. He was one of only a small handful of Labour Ministers to hold office under Harold Wilson, James Callaghan and Tony Blair. It is believed he did serve in the Welch Regiment as an officer and national serviceman. He was also Lord Lieutenant of Dyfed in 2002.

LEO ABSE

Leo Abse was one of the sons of Rudolph Abse, a Jewish solicitor and cinema owner who lived in Cardiff.

His maternal grandfather had emigrated to Wales from a town in Poland, then located within the Russian Empire. He attended Howard Gardens High School in Cardiff and then the London School of Economics where he studied law.

Having joined the Labour Party in 1934 he did visit Spain during the closing months of the Spanish Civil War. During the Second World War he served in the Royal Air Force and helped to set up a Forces Parliament to debate the structure of society they wanted see in the post war world. Senior officers forced the Parliament to be dissolved, and Abse was arrested for controversial views. He stood for Pontypool and won the seat. He was known as a character in the House of Commons and dressed flamboyantly on Budget day. In 1963 he introduced the Matrimonial Causes bill, which simplified and made easier the legal process of divorce. He helped found the All Party Parliamentary Humanist Group, which was concerned with homosexual law reform, abortion law reform and racial and religious equality. In 1957 the Wolfenden Report had recommended that the law be changed to decriminalize consenting male homosexual sex. Abse became the main sponsor to promote this legislation and the bill finally came to the statute book as the Sexual Offences Act 1967.

He was an opponent of devolution and chaired the select committee on abortion from 1975-1977. he strongly urged that British Forces should be removed from Northern Ireland, he opposed nuclear power and nuclear weapons and was against the Falklands War. He supported British membership of the European Communities. He wrote a book called *'Tony Blair, the Man who lost his Smile'* and in part of the book he claimed he paid off a blackmailer who had been targeting a fellow Welsh MP, George Thomas on the basis of Thomas's closet homosexuality.

A bust of Abse was unveiled at the National Museum of Wales on 22nd October 2009. In 1983 he had been elected for the renamed seat of Torfaen but retired from Parliament in 1987. He was certainly a maverick, but one with a liberal conscience.

ANN CLWYD

Ann Clwyd is the daughter of Gwilym Henry Lewis and Elizabeth Ann Lewis, born and brought up in Pentre Halkwy, Flintshire. She was educated at Holywell Grammar School and the Queen's School, Chester, before graduating from the University of Wales, Bangor. She was a student teacher at Hope School, Flintshire before training as a journalist. She then worked for BBC Wales as a studio manager and after that became Welsh correspondent for the Guardian and Observer newspapers during 1964-79. From 1979–84 she was the member of the European Parliament for mid and west Wales. She was elected to parliament in a by-election in May 1984 and became the first woman to sit for a Welsh Valleys constituency.

She served as Shadow Minister of Education and Womens Rights from 1987 but was sacked in 1988 for rebelling against the party whip on further spending on nuclear weapons. She returned as Shadow Minister for Overseas Development from 1989–1992 and then served as Shadow Secretary of State for Wales in 1992. She became Opposition Spokesperson for Foreign Affairs from 1994–1995 when she was again sacked for observing the Turkish Invasion of Iraqui Kirkuk without permission. In 1994 she staged a sit down in Tower Colliery in her constituency to protest at its closure.

Ann Clwyd

In her last years in Parliament, she was chair of the All Party Parliamentary Human Rights group and she was also Vice chair of the All Party Parliamentary group on Coal Field Communities and secretary of the All Party Parliamentary Group on Cambodia.

In a series of Parliamentary votes on 'Brexit' in March 2019, Clwyd voted against the Labour Party whip and in favour of an amendment tabled by members of the Independent group for a second public vote. On the question of Iraq, she was totally against the cruelties of the Saddam Hussein regime. She wrote an article in the Times outlining some of Saddam's cruelty and the Sun's political editor wrote in February 2004 that as a result of Clwyds article, public opinions swung behind Tony Blair as voters learned 'How Saddam fed dissidents feet first into industrial shredders'. Tony Blair made her a special envoy on Human Rights in Iraq in the run up to the war. Even after the Chilcot enquiry in February 2010 she said she would still have voted in Parliament in 2003 to support military action in Iraq.

She was a member of the Royal Commission on the National Health Service 1976-79 and in December 2012 publicly criticised the standard of nursing care that her husband Owen Roberts received at the University Hospital of Wales when he was dying there in October 2012. She focused on the lack of compassion shown to him.

In 2013 she was appointed by the Prime Minister to advise on complaint handling. She was made a Privy Counsellor and was admitted to the White Robe of the Gorsedd of Bards at the National Eisteddfod of Wales in 1991. She is an Honorary Fellow of the University of Wales Bangor.

LORD ELYSTAN MORGAN

Morgan was educated at Ardwyn Grammar school Aberystwyth and became a member of Plaid Cymru as a schoolboy in 1946. He studied law at the University College of Wales Aberystwyth where he was involved with student politics. He qualified as a solicitor and joined a legal firm in Wrexham. In 1955 he was adopted as a Plaid Cymru candidate and lost a couple of elections in Wrexham. However, he switched parties, joining the Labour Party and was elected Member of Parliament for Cardiganshire at the 1966 General Election. From 1968-70 he was under-secretary at the Home Office. He was a vigorous supporter of devolution, believing that Cardiff should have all major governing powers over Wales. But he lost his seat in February 1974 at the General Election. He sought election in 1979 for Anglesey but was defeated by Conservative candidate Keith Best.

Following this defeat, he largely withdrew from political life and concentrated on his legal career. He was created a Life Peer in May 1981 and held the office of circuit judge between 1987-2003. On 6th March 2007 he supported the abolition of the blasphemy law in the UK. He retired from the House of Lords in February 2020.

MERLYN REES

He was born in Cilfynydd near Pontypridd Glamorgan. His father was a war veteran who moved from Wales to England to find work. He was educated at Harrow Weald Grammar School and Goldsmiths College London. In 1941 he joined the Royal Air Force becoming a squadron leader and earning the nickname 'Dagwood'. He served in Italy as operations and intelligence officer to the No 324 Squadron. He then went on to become a schoolmaster in his old school at Harrow. He was unostentatiously proud of his roots, unending generations of Welsh miners. At a by-election in 1963 he stood successfully as Labour candidate for Leeds South, succeeding Gaitskell in the same year. He held the seat until he stepped down from the House of Commons at the 1992 General Election.

When the Labour government returned to power in March 1974, he was appointed secretary of state to Northern Ireland. He lifted the proscription against the illegal loyalist paramilitary organisation the Ulster Volunteer Force. He had to rescind this after their involvement in the Dublin bombings. He allowed the Sunningdale power sharing arrangements to collapse in Northern Ireland and was later almost assassinated by the IRA in July 1976.

Rees belonged to the Labour mainstream. A conventional politician perhaps, but a kindly very generally liked one whose ruminative reasonable style deflected criticism. Labour in it's travails

105

after Mrs Thatcher's second victory could rely on him for absolute loyalty, continuity and sense. In September 1976 he was appointed Home Secretary and remained in that post until Labour's defeat in the 1979 election.

He got on with most people, in particular with his Conservative opposite number Willie Whitelaw.

The greatest strengths of Rees as a politician were perhaps seen after he and Labour left office. The period 1979-81 were the darkest in labour's history. The outbursts of feral leftism at party conference, the restructuring of the election process into an instrument to create left domination, the defeat of Dennis Healey by Michael Foot for the leadership and then the destructive campaign for the deputy leadership by Tony Benn, all culminated in the breakout from the party by 30 sitting MPs and other notables and the creation of the Social Democrat Party. He was strong in persuading many to stay in the party. Not an inspirational or dominant figure, Rees was perfectly representative of the sensible, conscienced stable people by whom government is sustained.

THE MOVE TO THE ASSEMBLY

RON DAVIES

Ron Davies was born on 6th August 1946. He is a former Secretary of State for Wales, former Member of Parliament and a former Member of the Welsh Assembly. He describes himself as a politician belonging to the traditional left who had spent his life 'Looking for a socialist progressive party'. He is often said to have been the architect of devolution and then the campaign to create the National Assembly for Wales.

He resigned from Tony Blairs Cabinet in 1998 following what became known as 'a moment of madness' when he was mugged at knifepoint after agreeing to go for a meal with a man he had met at the well-known gay meeting place of Clapham Common. As the Labour Party's chief spokesman for Wales from 1992 to 1997 Davies developed the party's devolution policy. After he was appointed Secretary of State for Wales in 1997, one of his first acts was to return the £150,000 to the Aberfan Disaster Fund that a previous Labour government had taken to restore the site of the landslide that had devastated the Valley community in 1966, although inflation was not taken into account. He led the successful Labour party campaign for a yes vote in the devolution referendum on 18th September 1997 though the tiny majority in the referendum did not reinforce the institution's authority. He steered the Government of Wales bill through Parliament and on 31st July 1998 he saw the Government of Wales act reach the statute book.

For his achievement he was appointed to the highest order of the Gorsedd of the Bards at the 1998 National Eisteddfod in Bridgend. On 30th January 1999 he was selected as a Labour candidate for the first elections for the National Assembly. He was elected on 6th May 1999 as Assembly Member for the Caerphilly constituency. He is known for the phrase 'Devolution is a process and not an event'.

Shortly before the 2003 Assembly elections The Sun revealed that Davies had been visiting a well-known cruising spot near a motorway lay-by. When challenged as to what he had been doing, he told reporters that he had been going for a short walk and added, 'I have actually been there when I have been watching badgers'. Davies was forced by his local party to stand down as Labour candidate at the election.

He resigned from the Labour Party in 2004 and subsequently joined the new Forward Wales Party and stood for election to the European Parliament in June 2004 but failed to be elected. He then started supporting Plaid Cymru and stood as one of its candidates but was defeated in the 2011 election. Despite his setbacks it was his energy and application that brought the National Assembly into being.

RHODRI MORGAN

by Robin Lewis, advisor to the Welsh Government

Rhodri Morgan

108

'One of our nations giants'. With those words, then First Minister Carwyn Jones closed his tribute to his predecessor.

Indeed, the heartfelt accolades paid from all parties within the National Assembly for Wales to Rhodri Morgan following his death in May 2017 spoke of someone who had achieved that rare distinction in politics of being genuinely liked and admired by all sides. Speakers mentioned his ferocious intellect and remarkable memory, his integrity and sense of humour, his passionate campaigning and empathy with others.

Rhodri was a fully rounded human being with a wide hinterland who could connect with people with ease. Moreover, as Assembly Members who both supported and opposed Rhodris political vision attested, his was perhaps the defining role in making permanent a devolution settlement that had not had the easiest of births. Rhodris own birth, on 29th September 1939, was overshadowed by the start of the Second World War.

Born and brought up in Radyr, the Cardiff suburb he would later represent in both the House of Commons and the Welsh Assembly, Rhodris eponymous and posthumously published autobiography describes a childhood shaped by British, European and global influences. No less important were present and past Welsh influences. His parents, miners son and future Professor of Welsh, Thomas John Morgan and shopkeeper's daughter and former secondary school teacher Huana Rees, came from adjoining villages in the Lower Swansea Valley and met when studying for degrees in Welsh at the University College of Swansea. After degrees from Oriel College, Oxford and Harvard, Rhodri worked as a tutor-organiser at the Workers' Educational Association and then went on to hold posts in local and central government, ending up as Head of the European Commission for Wales. He had been an active member of the Labour Party since the 1960s, through which he met his future wife Julie, who likewise went on to serve in both UK and Welsh Parliaments.

Selected as Labour candidate for Cardiff West, at the 1987 General Election Rhodri gained the seat from the Conservatives which he would go on to represent for the next 24 years. Rhodri remained in the House of Commons until 2001. He joined the front bench a year after his election but, despite supporting Tony Blair in the Labour leadership election, was one of the Shadow Ministers not appointed to office after the 1997 election landslide. Instead, and as consolation, Rhodri became Chair of the House of Commons Public Administration Committee, a post which enabled him to take on the role of critical friend in a wide-ranging capacity across the Blair Governments remit.

Rhodri had played a key role in shaping Labour's position on devolution during the long years in opposition and had campaigned strongly for Welsh devolution in 1997. It was no surprise when he stood for election to what was then the Welsh Assembly in 1999. Those first elections to the devolved Parliament were sobering for Labour, with the loss of many seats perceived to be safe such as Islwyn and Rhondda. The end result saw Labour with just 28 out of 60 seats under the hybrid voting system in place.

One bright moment was Rhodris own election, as he resoundingly won his formerly marginal constituency with the largest majority of any Labour candidate. Incoming First Secretary Alun Michael duly formed a Labour Government. Rhodri joined Michaels Cabinet with responsibility for Economic Development and European Affairs, a post in which he described himself as being as 'happy as a bunny rabbit'.

Lacking an overall majority, the Welsh Assembly government faced a difficult time from opposition parties. Matters came to a head nine months later, as Michael faced a vote of no confidence tabled in the joint names of the leaders of Plaid Cymru, the Welsh Conservatives and the Welsh Liberal Democrats. The cause was the failure of Michael to gain agreement from the UK Government to provide match-funding for Objective 1 regional development money from the European Union. In the face of this concerted effort, Michael dramatically submitted his resignation as First Secretary and leader of Welsh Labour, resigning his Assembly seat shortly afterwards. Rhodri duly succeeded him, being confirmed as the only choice of the Welsh Cabinet, the Labour Assembly Members and the Party's Welsh Executive Committee, and the only formal nomination as First Secretary the following week.

The apparent unanimity through which Rhodri became leader of the Labour Party in Wales and First Secretary belies the convoluted route by which he succeeded to both roles. For in fact, this was Rhodri's third tilt at the crown. Rhodri had first stood to become Labour's nominee to lead the Welsh Assembly back in 1998. His opponent then was Caerphilly MP and Secretary of State for Wales Ron Davies and under the electoral college system in place, Davies won with over two thirds of the vote. He stood the second time after Davies had resigned following his 'moment of madness' on Clapham Common. Fellow Cardiff MP Alun Michael had succeeded Davies at the Welsh Office and then succeeded him as Labour nominee, beating Rhodri narrowly by 53% to 47%.

Controversially, Rhodri had won the party member section of the electoral college by two to one but lost in the trade union and elected politician sections. In both elections, there was the definite impression of Rhodri as idiosyncratic outsider struggling against the party hierarchy and not least of all against the influence Prime Minister Blair could bring to bear. Rhodri served in his new roles for more than nine years, retiring from the re-styled post of First Minister at a time of his own choosing in December 2009.

During this time, Welsh Labour under his stewardship remained in government in the Welsh Assembly. In the 2003 election, the party gained those constituencies disastrously lost, to end up with 30 Assembly Members out of 60. In 2007, there was a slight loss of constituencies, but Rhodri formed the One Wales coalition government with Plaid Cymru. This was the second such arrangement, as Rhodri had previously led a coalition with the Welsh Liberal Democrats during that first term when a majority was lacking. Distinctly Welsh Labour achievements of his term in office included the creation of the first Children's Commissioner post in the UK, and in Wales the removal of prescription charges, the introduction of a public smoking ban, the rejection of the PFI model of infrastructure spend and the provision of free school breakfasts for primary school children.

Two key developments of this period are worth briefly considering. The first relates to what may be considered as the overall philosophy of the devolved government, which was to adopt a more citizen-focused approach to public service delivery as opposed to the consumer and choice-based model being pushed by Blair's government in Westminster. For example, semi-autonomous foundation hospitals and academies were being pushed in the fields of health and education in England. Both were firmly rejected as models to follow in Wales in favour of made-in-Wales, public service focussed solutions. This became known as 'Clear Red Water', after a phrase included but not delivered in an influential speech by Rhodri at the National Centre for Public Policy in Swansea in 2002. The second relates to the extent to which Rhodri's leadership helped embed the concept of devolution within Wales.

The fledgling democracy that had been established in 1999 did struggle, but it was strengthened after Rhodri assumed office. This can be shown by comparing the two recent referendums on devolution in Wales. The 1997 referendum on establishing the Welsh Assembly had been won by a little over 6,000 votes across the entire country.

The referendum in 2011 on giving the Welsh Assembly full law-making powers, a consequence of that One Wales agreement in 2007, was won by nearly 220,000 votes. Allied to this, this process of stabilisation was key to enabling Welsh democracy to mature and transform to become the system we have in place today. Rhodri left the Welsh Assembly at the 2011 election. He served as Chancellor of Swansea University and adjusted well to a life beyond politics. He had undergone heart surgery in 2007 but remained active until his death on 17th May 2017 whilst out cycling.

This essay opened with the tribute of Rhodri Morgans successor as First Minister. To close, it seems appropriate to quote the words of his successor in turn, Mark Drakeford, who had for many years been one of Rhodris closest political allies. 'The devolution journey we have all been on would have been very different, and far, far more difficult if not for Rhodri Morgan'.

THE LIBERALS AND LIBERAL DEMOCRATS

The Liberals in the 19th century were the natural party of Wales, being anti landowner and the representatives of non-conformism. Up to the time when Lloyd George split the Liberal Party in the early part of the 20th century, they were quite dominant in Wales. They represented the majority of the 28 constituencies. After the electoral reforms, Wales went up to 40 constituencies, but most of those became Labour. It is only now with the possible increase in Assembly numbers and another bout of electoral reform that Wales will lose a number of MPs. It seems unlikely to the author that we will ever have another Welsh Prime Minister because of these numbers.

THE DAVIESES OF LLANDINAM

David Davies the industrialist was the eldest of 9 children; he was self-educated and began work as a sawyer and went into agriculture. He became successful and took over a number of farms. He soon built a reputation as a contractor and built many roads and bridges, and also railway lines. His greatest achievement was the section of the Manchester/Milford Haven railway from Pencader to Aberystwyth which opened in 1867.

The most difficult part was the crossing of Tregaron Bog. It is said that he bought up the entire year's production of sheep fleeces in Ceredigion to lay as a foundation for the railway over the bog.

He stood for election to Parliament as a Liberal and was up against the vested interests of the landowners. He used his commercial acumen which included depositing £10,000 in an Aberystwyth bank as they owed money for the battle. He finally got into Parliament in 1874 and remained there until 1886.

Having been very successful in the railway trade, he took a chance at digging coal in the Rhondda where, after some time without

114

success, he ran out of money but his men thought so much about him as an employer that they worked on for another week and found one of the classic seams of coal in that valley.

By the 1880s, the output from his collieries had increased to such an extent that Davies established a limited liability company, The Ocean Coal Company Ltd. However, the huge expensive costs were getting his coal to the Bute Docks in Cardiff and Davies got round this by building new docks at Barry, with a railway connection from the Rhondda. At the time of his death in 1890, Ocean Coal was the largest and most profitable coal company in South Wales. By upbringing he was a Calvanistic Methodist, he was a teetotaller and very determined about his Sunday observance. He was a keen patron of the new university at Aberystwyth. He was elected as Liberal Member of Parliament for Cardigan Boroughs and held the seat until 1885, when he was elected for the Cardiganshire County seat. He was a poor public speaker but his success was partly due to the 13,000 members of the Calvanistic Methodist Denomination in Cardiganshire. He was defeated in the 1886 election after splitting with Gladstone over home rule for Ireland, but he lost the election by 9 votes and then withdrew from political life that same year.

After he died, he left his only child, Edward Davies who died of mental exhaustion in 1898. His grandson, another David Davies continued his grandfather's philanthropic activities and was elevated to the Peerage; 2 grandaughters, Gwendoline Davies and Margaret Davies donated their substantial art collection to the National Museum of Wales. In 1884 David Davies had bought the large country house Plasdinam where he died on 20th July 1890 aged 71.

David Davies, the industrialists grandson was MP for Montgomeryshire from 1906 until 1929. He had been educated at Merchiston Castle School and King's College Cambridge. At a young age his familys wealth allowed him to travel extensively to exotic locations where he enjoyed game hunting. In the 1st World War he commanded the 14th Battalion of the Royal Welsh Fusiliers until 1916 when he was appointed Parliamentary Secretary to David Lloyd George. Following the war, Davies became an active supporter of the

League of Nations and in 1929 he stood down prior to the General Election to focus on international affairs. He had already established the Edward VII Welsh National Memorial to combat tuberculosis in Wales, as well as the Wilson chair of International Politics at the University College of Wales Aberystwyth. He established the new Commonwealth Society for the promotion of international law and order. His ideas influenced the writing of the United Nations Charter, especially with regards to sanctions, and usage of national armies as an international police. He was also the President of the National Library of Wales. The Chair of International Politics he established at Aberystwyth University was done in honour of Woodrow Wilson in 1919. In 1944 while launching a new X ray mobile scanning unit at Sully Hospital, Davies volunteered to undergo the first routine chest scan. The scan revealed advanced cancer from which he died a few months later in June 1944.

Davies was also the brainchild and leading funder of the Welsh Temple of Peace in Cardiff, pledging £58,000 in 1934, about £4.15 million in today's money, towards the erection of a building. He had 6 children altogether through 2 wives.

Even today, the Davieses are a philanthropic family. There has been a perception that most of the coal owners in Wales were from England. This was quite wrong, for over 50 per cent of them were Welsh and the greatest of them all was David Davies.

THE LIBERALS IN MONTGOMERYSHIRE

The record of continuous Liberal and Liberal Democrat representation with one break of 4 years, runs for 130 years from 1880 to 2010. Before that in the country constituency seat at least, there was almost continuous Conservative or Tory representation. The urban craft of weaving and spinning generated some radical politics, including giving birth to Robert Owen, the only pioneer of the Cooperative movement. Welshpool was dominated by Montgomeryshire's most aristocratic family for 100 years, namely the Herberts into whose family Clive of India married. The late 19th century saw the rise of new merchants like David Davies ('Top Sawyer') the Liberal MP who'd made his fortune in coal mining in South Wales and built Barry Docks. The countryside was littered with small tenant farmers who had few rights and although many were chapel goers, they paid their tithes to the church and their tolls to the toll owners. The Reform Act of 1867 doubled the electorate adding in many tenant farmers.

Rendel the MP at the time became something of a hero. After he was elected many of the grievances he'd fought came to a head, such as tithe reform, disestablishment, landlord and tenant relations and the abolition of tolls. David Davies, grandson of the David Davies of Barry Docks fame, served in the 1st World War and became an MP. Emlyn Hooson became one of the most prominent MPs of the time. The extraordinary thing is that the radical tradition of the 1880s and the 1890s lasted for so long and it's only in the last 20 or so years that Montgomeryshire has begun to reject its radical tradition. Lembit Opik was probably the beginning of the decline. It was difficult for the people of that county to take him seriously.

EMLYN HOOSON

Emlyn Hooson was born at Colomendy in Denbighshire and was

educated at Denbigh Grammar School and read law at the University of Wales in Aberystwyth. He joined the Royal Navy in 1943 and served during the 2nd World War on a Corvette in the north Atlantic.

He became a barrister called to the bar by Gray's Inn in 1949, and in 1960 he became one of the youngest ever Queen's Counsel at age 35. As QC, Hooson represented Ian Brady, one of the Moors murderers along with Myra Hindley. He went on the become recorder both of Merthyr Tydfil and Swansea in 1971 and was elected leader of the Wales and Chester circuit 1971-74. He was a recorder of the Crown Court from 1972 -1991 as well as a deputy High Court judge. As Chairman of the Liberal Party of Wales, he led its merger with the North and South Wales Liberal Federations, thereby uniting Liberalism in Wales in the Welsh Liberal Party.

He became MP for Montgomeryshire at a 1962 by election following the death of Clement Davies. He contested the Liberal Party leadership election of 1967 but withdrew in favour of Jeremy Thorpe. He voted against entry into the Common Market although he campaigned for a yes vote (with remain after it) in the 1975 Referendum. He introduced the Government of Wales bill on St David's Day in 1967 taking one of the first steps to the formation of the Welsh Assembly. He lost his seat to the Conservatives in the 1979 General Election and was then appointed a Peer. He sat for the Liberal Democrats in the House of Lords, where he was active in improving the Mental Health Act, and also backed Police reform and Law reform. In 1950 he had married Shirley Hamer, daughter of Sir George Hamer Lord Lieutenant of Montgomeryshire. In 1980 he became a member of the ITV Advisory Council. He became a non-executive director of Laura Ashley and was later made chairman in 1995. He was chairman of the trustees of the Laura Ashley Foundation from 1986-7 and became president of the National Eisteddfod of Wales at Newtown in 1996. He died on the 21st February 2012.

LORD GERAINT HOWELLS

He was a leading Welsh Liberal Democrat politician who was educated at Pontywyd Primary School and Ardwyn Grammar School Aberystwyth. His main living was that of a hill farmer and he held some 750 acres with around 3,000 sheep. The majority were prize winning speckle faces. He was also a champion sheep shearer. He was chairman of the Wool Producers of Wales 1977-83.

In 1972 he was elected as the Parliamentary candidate for Cardiganshire, a seat with a longstanding Liberal tradition. It had been held by the Liberal MP Roderick Bowen until his defeat by Labour's Elyston Morgan.

In the February 1974 General Election Howells defeated Morgan and retained the constituency in different forms until 1992. He was the Liberal Party spokesman on Welsh Affairs and Agriculture. It is interesting that one of his researchers in the House of Commons was Mark Williams who later won the seat for the Liberal Democrats in 2005. In 1992 Howells unexpectedly lost his seat to Plaid Cymru which formed an alliance with the Wales Green Party; this appealed greatly to the non Welsh speakers in the constituency.

He was a passionate pro devolutionist and played a lead role in the 1979 devolution campaign. He was also able to get the Farmers Union of Wales recognition as one of the official unions for government negotiations during the Lib-Lab pact in the 1970s. He was a very popular MP for some time and epitomised a typical Cardiganshire character with much appreciation from the countryside and farming community.

In the House of Lords, he was a great friend of Richard Livesey and Emlyn Hooson, who had also been stalwart Liberal MPs.

SIR SIMON HUGHES

Hughes was born on 17th May 1951 and educated at the Cathedral School Llandaff where he was Dean's Scholar and Head boy in 1964. The author got to know him at Christ College Brecon where Hughes became Head of School. He was an excellent chorister and also played a bit of rugby. He went to Selwyn College Cambridge where he graduated in law and the College of Europe in Bruges where he earned a post graduate certificate of Advanced European Studies. He was called to the Bar in the Inner Temple in 1974. He moved to Bermondsey in 1977. He was first elected to Parliament in the Bermondsey by -election of 24th February 1983 in which he defeated Labour candidate and gay rights campaigner Peter Tatchell. It was described as a very dirty campaign. Hughes went on to reveal his own bisexual experiences, however Hughes subsequently chose to abstain from the final vote for gay marriage.

He first joined the Liberal Party at Cambridge and as part of the SDP Liberal Democrat alliance he was spokesman for the Environment from 1983–1988. He joined the newly founded Liberal Democrats in 1988 and he was the Liberal Democrat candidate in the 2004 Mayor of London Elections. He lost that election. Many believe it was Hughes speech in a Liberal Party Conference that caused the Liberals to vote against an independent nuclear deterrent. He was a member of the Centre Left Liberal group within the Liberal Democrats. In December 2013 he became Minister of State for Justice. He was appointed a Privy Counsellor in 2010 and was knighted for public and political service in 2015. He became Deputy Leader in 2010 defeating Tim Farron by 38 votes to 18.

He has twice run unsuccessfully for the leadership of the Liberal Democrats and is at the time of writing the Chancellor of London South Bank University. He was Deputy leader of the Liberal Democrats from 2010–2014, and from 2013 until 2015 was Minister of State at the Ministry of Justice.

He was the Member of Parliament for the constituency of Bermondsey and Old Southwark from 1983–2015. Ever since the author knew him at school he was dedicated to the cause of justice and always had goodwill with those people who had had a difficult life. He is a great Christian and showed this quality in his Parliamentary career.

THE LIBERALS OF BRECON & RADNOR

RICHARD LIVSEY

Baron Livsey of Talgarth

He served as Member of Parliament for Brecon and Radnor from 1985– 1992 and again from 1997-2001.

He was the son of Arthur Norman Livsey and Lilian Maisie. His father was a sea captain who died in Iraq when Richard was just 3 years old. He was therefore brought up in a single parent household by his mother Lilian who was a local teacher and headmistress. She had a great influence on his life. He was educated at Talgarth County Primary School, Bedales School, Seale-Hayne Agricultural College and Reading University.

He married Irene Yearsman of Castle Douglas, Galloway, Scotland and they went on to have 2 sons and a daughter. He was an agricultural development officer for ICI from 1961-67 and then became the farm manager on the Blairdrummond Estate in Perthshire from 1967-1971. He returned to Wales as a senior lecturer in the Welsh Agricultural College until 1975. In 1970, he stood unsuccessfully as the Liberal Party Scottish candidate in Perth and East Perthshire. When he returned to Wales, he stood unsuccessfully for Pembroke in 1979. He was a keen supporter and activist during the 1979 St David's Day Referendum on the Welsh Assembly on behalf of the Yes Campaign and became one of the most prominent promoters of the devolution referendum. He won the Brecon and Radnor by-election as a Liberal in 1985 with a majority of 559. This election was a great success for the Liberals. With his background in farm management, he joined Parliaments Select Committee on Agriculture.

He held his seat in 1987 becoming the Liberal Democrat spokesman on Wales and held the position as leader of the party in

Wales from 1988-1992. He lost the seat at the 1992 election by the narrow margin of 130 votes but regained it again at the 1997 General Election with a majority of over 5,000. He had built the Liberal Democrats in B&R to a formidable position which enabled Kirsty Williams the Assembly Member and his successor Roger Williams to further stretch the Liberal Democrat hold there. Richard Livsey was an extremely nice man who loved Wales and his constituency; he was patron of many organisations in Brecon and Radnor including the Hay Festival, chairman of the Brecon Jazz Festival and a member of the Talgarth Male Voice Choir. He was succeeded by Roger Williams at the 2001 UK General Election and was created a Life Peer on 28th August 2001.

He died on 16th September 2010 aged 75.

There is no doubt he was a great constituency MP.

ROGER WILLIAMS MP

Roger Williams was MP for Brecon & Radnor from 2001-2015.

He was born in the town of Crickhowell and studied at Christ College Brecon and Selwyn College Cambridge. He joined the Labour Party in 1969 but left to join the SDP at the formation of the party in 1981. He represented it and subsequently the Liberal Democrats on Powys County Council. In 1990 he was elected chairman of Brecon Beacons National Park. In 2001 he was elected MP to represent the constituency of Brecon & Radnor with a majority of 751 following the retirement of fellow Liberal Democrat Richard Livsey.

At the 2005 Election he was returned with an improved majority of 3,905. He served as Shadow Welsh Secretary in the Liberal Democrat front bench team in the 2005–2010 Parliament and was re-elected at the 2010 Election with a majority of 3,747. He was chairman of the Brecon & Radnor National Farmers Union and board member of the Wales-Agri Food Partnership. He was vice chairman of the Trading & Enterprise Council for Powys and Mid

Wales and was on the Development Board for Rural Wales.

Personally, he loved reading, walking, cricket and rugby. As an MP his work on local issues included campaigns for better contingency planning to deal with bird flu, disclosure of membership of closed societies, and he was also keen on red phone boxes and rural broadband. He campaigned against identity cards. He was a Member of the House of Commons Science and Technology Committee. He was an office holder of the all-party groups on agriculture and food for development, conservation and wildlife, Gurkha welfare and National Parks. In 2003 he participated in the Parliamentary Armed Forces scheme and was seconded into the army for a year.

Roger was a very shrewd politician behind a mask of great affability, keeping his seat for 3 elections but by the 4th when he lost it the nature of his seat of his seat had changed and there were far more people coming in from outside who had money and were therefore more likely to vote Conservative. He was always a kind-hearted man who was prepared to listen to people's troubles and advise them and was quick to act and help if he could. During his time as an MP the Liberal home ground of non-conformity and small farmers was somewhat undermined by changes in demography. So he eventually lost his last election but stayed in public life as a County Councillor. He is a man who has given over the years a lot to his community and remains much respected.

KIRSTY WILLIAMS

Kirsty Williams was born on 19th March 1971. She was a Member of the Senedd from 1999 to 2021. The author didn't vote for her at first to become Assembly Member for Brecon & Radnor because he thought she wasn't 'tough enough' to be a politician. How wrong he was! He didn't realise that she traced her family back to the line of Oliver Cromwell née Williams.

Kirsty Williams

She was educated at the independent St Michael's school Llanelli and studied at the Victoria University at Manchester where she obtained an honours degree in American Studies including a time studying at the University of Missouri. She joined the Welsh Liberal Democrats at the age of 15 and was a hugely keen supporter for the creation of a Welsh Assembly and she was appointed to the National Assembly Advisory Group by Welsh Secretary Ron Davies.

In her first term at the Senedd she became her party's health spokesperson. She also served as chair of the Welsh Assembly Health and Social Care Committee.

In a poll at the end of 2006, she was voted 'The sexiest female

Liberal Democrat' on Stephen Tall's 'Liberal goes a long way' blog. In 2011 as leader of the Welsh Liberal Democrats she agreed to support the Welsh Labour Governments 2012-2013 Budget. One of the concessions she achieved was the Welsh Pupil Premium, an extra £20 million to spend on the education of the poorest pupils. In 2013 the Welsh Liberal Democrats more than doubled investment for the Welsh Pupil Premium in exchange for abstaining on the Welsh Government's annual budget.

She had a reputation for campaigning on health issues. In 2013 the Welsh Liberal Democrats achieved a further £9.5 million investment into the Health Technology Fund. She was given leave to proceed with her bill in 2014 requiring a minimum nurse staffing levels in Welsh hospitals.

In 2016 she stood down as Leader of the Welsh Liberal Democrats after the election. Under her leadership it had not been a very successful time for the Liberal Democrats in Wales, partly because of the unpopular coalition with the Conservatives.

After the Election in 2016 as the sole Lib Dem representative in the Assembly she voted with the government on the appointment of the First Minister Carwyn Jones. She was appointed by him to be Education Secretary which gave him the extra seat Labour wanted for a working majority.

She has been at the forefront of curriculum reform in Wales and introduced the Curriculum and Assessment Wales bill on 6th July 2020. On 27th October 2020 she announced she would not be seeking re-election in the 2021 Senedd election. She could see the writing on the wall and an upsurge in Conservative popularity in Brecon and Radnor. Some criticised her for going in with a Labour government but it did give the Liberals much more influence than if she had stayed as the sole Liberal Democrat outside a Labour Government.

She is a remarkable politician with huge stamina and insight and did well despite her party's low popularity in Wales.

PLAID CYMRU OVER THE YEARS

The party has had huge attraction in their heartlands of the north and west but has not made a lot of progress out of these.

In cooperating with the Labour Party in the Assembly they have had a great deal of influence on policy.

SAUNDERS LEWIS

John Saunders Lewis was an Englishman by birth. He was born in Wallasey in Cheshire on 15th October 1893, the second son of the Rev Lodwig Lewis, a native of Llanarthne in Carmarthanshire, Minister of the Welsh Calvinistic Methodist Church in Liskeard Road, Wallasey and his wife Mary Margaret. His education was entirely English. His father gave him some advice as a student and said, 'Look here Saunders, nothing will come of you until you come back to your roots.' His father would not tolerate any English being spoken in the house and Saunders spent the summer holidays with his mothers Welsh-speaking family on a farm in Anglesey.

Saunders Lewis

On leaving school, Saunders Lewis went to study English and French at the University of Liverpool. During this time, he was inspired to start reading Welsh literature and he was very influenced by the sense of deep Welsh patriotism in a European setting displayed by T Gwynn Jones who wrote the biography of Emrys ap Iwan in 1912. Even at this time he was very impressed by the Catholic and Latin tradition in Wales before the Protestant Reformation. He was also a great reader of Anglo-Irish literature and was one of the few Welsh people who gave the Easter Rising his support.

In 1914, after he had spent a couple of years at Liverpool, the First World War broke out and in his own words, 'As a good British patriot I felt quite happy to volunteer to stop bullying Germany's attack on Belgium'. He joined the South Wales Borderers Regiment as a soldier. After nine months he was promoted to officer which was unusual for the Welsh speaking volunteers were very seldom promoted. On arriving in France with the 12th (3rd Gwent) S W Borderers (Bantam) battalion he found the French people delightful and on 14th June 1916 the battalion went into the trenches. He was sent to hospital in Boulogne suffering from trench fever. On return to a new sector (Maroc) he was involved in patrolling and displayed some gallantry in attacking the Seaforth Crater which was recognised by the Brigade staff. During November, the Borderers marched southwards until, in late September, they went into trenches in the Rancourt sector of the Somme. This was the most miserable countryside and the weather was awful; it was very cold and there was a huge amount of mud everywhere.

He wrote to his friend and later wife, Margaret Gilchrist, that, 'I can't hope to describe to you the mixture of horror and grotesque humour of this line. Nothing at all of what I have seen before of trench warfare was at all like this. In the line we held we were in shell holes waist high in slime without even the semblance of a trench. Dead men were as common as the living. They had died in all kinds of positions. Numbers had merely drowned. Until your attitude towards them became one of mingled tenderness and sympathy and humorous acceptance one joked with them and often joined them'.

The Germans began their retirement to the Hindenburg line on 14th March. For three weeks the 12th S W Borderers worked on building railway lines. After this work, the 40th Division, in which they were, came up to the Hindenburg line and were ordered to mount a great assault. Saunders Lewis was wounded in the left thigh and calf; two machine gun bullets went through the knee and a piece of shrapnel blew the calf of his leg away about an hour later. During his time in France he lost his younger brother Lodwig, and it appears that his war years were quite traumatic for him. Although he once said they were the best years of his life.

In 1918 he was sent to Athens and served as a personal guard to the Prime Minister where he remained until the end of the war and where he had plenty of time to read and think. He returned to Wales a nationalist. He went on to reject socialism and believed in a sort of aristocracy immersed in the culture of language who should run Wales. He rejected pacifism and the temperance movement. He had great respect for those who soldiered for their courage and bravery and he himself loved fine food and wine. In 1922 he was appointed head of the department of Welsh at the new University of Wales, Swansea. In a Non-conformist, proletariat and socialist Wales, he was a Catholic elitist and believed in aristocracy. In January 1924 together with two other contemporary Welsh intellectuals he founded at Penarth a secret society known as 'Y Mudiad Cymrag' the 'Welsh Movement' which became the National Party of Wales. In 1926 he was elected president and he remained in office until 1939. The National Party's aim was dominion status for Wales, self-government under British sovereignty.

At the root of Saunders Lewis's politics was a spirituality which certainly governed his attitude towards his country. As far back as 1923 Saunders Lewis had said, 'it would be a great blessing for Wales if some Welshman did something for his nation that would result in his imprisonment'. In 1936 the opportunity arose. The Ministry of War were determined to put a training camp and associated aerodrome at Porth Neigwl on the Lleyn Peninsula. Saunders Lewis was against it because he said it would grow and spread. He said it was a holy place and the threat was aimed directly and unfailingly at the heart and life of our language, our literature and our existence as a nation. Some five hundred different organisations protested against the bombing school. Baldwin, the Prime Minister, rejected the protests.

About half past one on the morning of Tuesday 8th September 1936 the Rev. Lewis Valentine, DJ Williams and Saunders Lewis set fire to the sheds, the offices and the building material that the Cowsin company had set up at the Penyberth site. They walked into a police station and admitted what they had done. They were arrested and charged with malicious damage. After the first trial was adjourned because the jury failed to agree, a second one was heard at the King's Bench at the Central Court in London. This time a resounding 'guilty' was given by the mainly English jurors. They were sentenced to nine months imprisonment in Wormwood Scrubs.

Saunders found it difficult to get a job after his prison sentence but, in 1941, he published his only volume of poetry, 'Byd y Betws'. He said, 'To the world belongs all materialism and everything sordid and base; to the church belongs everything civilised including the Welsh language tradition.' Two of his poems, 'Mair Fadlyn' and 'Marwnad Syr John Edward Lloyd' are said to be two of the best poems to have been written in Welsh. He was deprived of a lectureship at the University of Wales for a period of fifteen years.

In 1952 he applied for a post in the Welsh department at the University of Wales College, Cardiff and was appointed. He remained there until his retirement in 1957. On 13th February 1962, at the invitation of the BBC, he delivered his hugely important lecture on the fate of the language. He also saw, with current trends continuing, that the Welsh language would die out around the start of the 21st century. The lecture had an immediate influence on the younger generation in Wales, who brought a Welsh element to the global protest movement of the 1960s and the Welsh Language Society was founded on 4th August 1962 and in 1963 Saunders Lewis was its first honorary president.

130

He died on 1st September 1985, and then it was revealed that in 1975 Pope Paul VI had honoured him with the title of 'Knight Commander of the Order of St Gregory the Great'.

There is not a lot to say about his relationships with other men and officers in the trenches but he does say in one letter, 'I shall never forget it. I shall never forget the faces, the stooping backs or the songs that expressed so much mens desires, mens longings and mens grossness, most of them loveable things.' In another letter to Margaret on June 11th ,1915 he talks about, 'being put in charge of the scouts and signalling sections of our battalion. I was sent to instruct them and, as there is a great deal of writing to do in these tasks, I soon discovered that a big proportion of the men is quite illiterate and that to read, write and spell proficiently is quite exceptional, so I have set out to form a night school in the battalion.'

When it comes to war he talks about, 'The waste of richness and goodness, the vandalism of it all. Even if there were no blood spilt, and no actual ugliness, no positive evil or loss one gains nothing by it.' Saunders Lewis was one of the great Welsh intellectuals of the 20th century.

It seems sad that in the South Wales Borderers Museum in Brecon there is little mention of him despite his bravery as a captain in that regiment in the First World War. Although he was small in stature, he was a man of great style. He was never boring. Unlike his close friend David Jones, he wrote next to nothing about the war and we have very little of what his contemporaries thought of him or he of them but his personality was a dichotomy. He was, at once, a very private person but, at the same time, he became a very public personality. He didn't seem to bear any grudge about the class divisions in soldiering or any feeling of being exploited as a soldier.

He was, essentially, a man who stood up against bullies but felt himself belonging to something wider than a small nation. He was a European and became a Roman Catholic. He had a wider vision than the introspection of a small nationalist. He made a huge contribution to Wales and its culture and should be recognised for this.

'Saunders Lewis, a Presentation of his Work' by Harri Pritchard Jones

'Saunders Lewis, Selected Poems' translated by Joseph P Clancy

'The Story of Saunders Lewis, the Poet of Welsh Revolution' by Gwynn ap Gwilym

GWYNFOR EVANS

1 Sept 1912 – 21 April 2005

He was a Welsh politician, lawyer and author. He was President of Plaid Cymru for 36 years and was the first Member of Parliament to represent it at Westminster, which he did twice, from 1966-1970 and again from 1974-1979. He was born in Barry, where his father ran a chain of shops and his mother a china shop. He was educated at Barry County School, where he was captain of the school's cricket and hockey teams. Although he began learning the Welsh language at school, he did not become fully fluent until the age of 17.

He studied at the University of Wales Aberystwyth and at St John's College Oxford, from where he qualified as a lawyer. He was also a market gardener. He founded a branch of Plaid Cymru when he was at Oxford, although he was only a teenager when the party was founded in 1925. He was a committed Christian and was a conscientious objector. In the 1950s he campaigned unsuccessfully for a Welsh Parliament and failed to prevent the damming of the Tryweryn River and consequent inundation of the Welsh speaking community of Capel Cenyn to supply the City of Liverpool. It is interesting that although the vast majority of Welsh MPs were against this, they were overruled by Parliament at Westminster.

In July 1966, Evans won the Parliamentary seat of Carmarthen from Labour in a by-election caused by the death of Lady Megan Lloyd George, daughter of the former Liberal Prime Minister. This was a great moment for Plaid Cymru. In the General Election of October 1974, having lost the seat in the 1970 General Election he regained the seat with a majority of 3,640 votes. He lost Carmarthen again in the 1979 General Election to Dr Roger Thomas, Labour. He was unsuccessful in the 1983 General Election and did not contest any further elections.

In the 1974 General Election he returned to Parliament accompanied by two other Plaid Cymru MPs, Dafydd Wigley and Dafydd Elis-Thomas. In his career as MP, he followed his pacifist principles, especially against the war in Vietnam. In 1980 his threat to go on hunger strike after the Conservative government reneged on its promise of a Welsh language television channel was instrumental in bringing about an early U-turn on the part of Margaret Thatcher, and S4C began broadcasting on 1st November 1982. It is said that Lord Cledwyn and the Archbishop of Wales went to see Thatcher and said that if Gwynfor died on hunger strike, she would have another Northern Ireland on her hands. In political retirement he became a prolific writer and his book, 'Land of My Fathers, 2,000 Years of Welsh History' published in 1974 became a best seller.

His heart was very much attached to Wales. Some would say he was a very emotional man, but he always put Wales first. Like many of his colleagues he was for Welsh independence, and this today is not an unrealistic ambition. If Wales controlled its own water and developed fully it's alternative power sources, there is a possibility it could survive independence; after all, it is about the same size at Latvia and Lithuania.

DAFYDD WIGLEY

He served as Plaid Cymru Member of Parliament for Caernarfon from 1974 until 2001, and as Assembly Member for Caernarvon from 1999 until 2003. He was Leader of Plaid Cymru from 1981 to 1984 and again from 1991 to 2000. He was born in Derby, England, the only child of Welsh parents. He attended Caernarvon Grammar School and Rydal School before going on to the Victoria University of Manchester and training as an accountant. He was employed by Hoover as a financial controller before entering Parliament.

In 1974 he became one of Plaid Cymru's first three MPs to be elected to Parliament. He represented a moderate, pragmatic Social Democrat side of Plaid in sharp contrast with his rival candidate for president Dafydd Elis Thomas' left-wing Socialism. He married the international harpist Elinor Bennett and the couple had 4 children, son Hywel Wigley and daughter Eluned Wigley as well as 2 sons Alun and Geraint who both sadly died of a genetic illness. He took a strong interest in the affairs of disabled people and was vice president of MENCAP Wales and of Disability Wales.

On 19th November 2010 it was announced that he had been granted a Life Peerage by the Queen. It is interesting that even during his Presidency, he was on the back foot against the party's ideology which had moved to the left. As a person, the author got to know him quite well and felt he was a man of great integrity and openness. He was the acceptable face of nationalism.

DAFYDD ELIS-THOMAS

Thomas was a Welsh and Welsh speaking politician representing the Dwyfor Merioneth constituency in the Senedd. He was born in Carmarthen, raised in Ceredigion and the Conwy Valley. He represented Merioneth, then Merioneth Nant, Conwy constituencies as a Member of Parliament from 1974 until 1992 and was the Llywydd of the Senedd from its inception in 1999 to 2011. He is a member of the House of Lords, a former Leader of Plaid Cymru and, since 2004, Privy Counsellor. In 1970 he married Elen Williams and had three sons; they later divorced and in 1993 he married Mair Parry-Jones.

On 14th October 2016 he left Plaid Cymru in order to support the Welsh Government and then sat as an independent in the Senedd. He was the Deputy Minister for Culture, Sport and Tourism. He was also the Chairman of the Welsh Language Board between 1994 and 1999. A former university lecturer, he has been the President for Bangor University since 2000. He also held the position of presiding officer from the Assembly's start from 1999 until 2011. During this time as presiding officer, he expelled Assembly Member Leanne Wood from the Assembly chamber during a December 2004 debate after Wood referred to Queen Elizabeth II as 'Mrs Windsor' during a debate and refused to withdraw the remark. He announced on BBC Radio Cymru that he would not be standing in the next Senedd Election in 2021.

There is no doubt he has been a controversial figure, but his charismatic personality has made him known throughout Wales, and he has always had its people at heart.

ADAM PRICE

At present Adam Price is the latest Leader of Plaid Cymru and has many interesting ideas which he partly formulated from the perspective of Harvard University. He has a strong intellect and Plaid are waiting to see what impact he has on Wales.

Plaid has not had a huge effect on Wales and is very much restricted to the western reaches and North Wales. However it has hung on tenaciously to its Parliamentary seats and has a strong following in the Senedd. With the advent of 'Brexit' there may be greater calls for an independent Wales.

THE SOCIAL DEMOCRATIC PARTY

LORD DAVID OWEN

Owen was born in 1938 to Welsh parents in Plympton, near the city of Plymouth. He went to the public school Bradfield College in Berkshire and was then admitted to Sidney Sussex College Cambridge in 1956 to study medicine. He began clinical training in St Thomas's Hospital in 1959 and in 1960 he joined the Vauxhall branch of the Labour Party and the Fabian Society. In 1962 he began work at St Thomas's Hospital and he was for 2 years neurology and psychiatric registrar and also did work with Parkinsonian trauma.

In 1964 he stood for Labour in Torrington but did not win the seat. In the General Election in 1966 he was returned for Plymouth Sutton and in 1974 became Labour MP for Plymouth Devonport. From 1968 to 1970 he served as Parliamentary Secretary of State for the Navy in Harold Wilson's first government.

After Labour's defeat in 1970 he resigned over Labour's opposition to the European Community but on Labour's return to government in March 1974 he became Minister of State for Health. In 1976, in September, he was appointed by the new Prime Minister James Callaghan as the Minister of State at the Foreign Office. When Anthony Crossland died, Owen became the youngest Foreign Secretary (aged 38) since Anthony Eden in 1935. As Foreign Secretary he was involved with Rhodesia and wrote a book entitled, 'Human Rights'. After Labour's defeat in the 1979 General Election and Michael Foot came to power as the leader of the Labour Party, he brought more left-wing attitudes such as a commitment to withdraw from the EEC and also the endorsement of unilateral nuclear disarmament. Also, a 40% block in the electoral college for leadership elections for the trade unions. Then, early in 1981, Owen and 3 other senior moderate Labour politicians announced their intentions to break away from the Labour Party, and the council they formed became the Social Democratic Party. 28 other Labour MPs joined. In late 1981 the SDP formed an alliance with the Liberal Party. Owen challenged Roy Jenkins for the leadership of the SDP and was initially defeated but came back after the 1982 General Election. Unfortunately, although the Alliance got 25% of the vote in the election, because of the election system it only won 23 seats in the House of Commons. Owen managed to maintain the SDPs independence from the Liberals for the length of the 1983 Parliament. There were splits in 1984 and 1985 over the miners strike with the SDP favouring a tougher line than the Liberals. There were also splits over replacing the *Polaris* with *Trident*. In 1987, after an election, the Liberal leader David Steel proposed a full merger. Owen rejected this and was defeated.

After this time Owen became an outsider. He was made a member of the House of Lords as a Social Democrat and believed in that movement as represented in many European countries. He was for many years respected for his politics of conscience and is still very much alive today.

ROY JENKINS

Baron Jenkins of Hillhead

The son of Arthur Jenkins, a coal miner and Labour MP, Jenkins went to the University of Oxford and served as an intelligence officer in the 2nd World War.

He was initially elected as MP for Southwark Central in 1948, moving to become MP for Birmingham Stechford in 1950. After the election of Harold Wilson in 1964 he was appointed Minister of Aviation and a year later he was promoted to the Cabinet to become Home Secretary. He was a great reformer and sought to build a civilised society, overseeing measures such as the effective abolition in Britain of both capital punishment and theatre censorship, the partial decriminalisation of homosexuality, relaxing of the divorce law, suspension of birching, and the liberalisation of abortion law.

Roy Jenkins

After the great devaluation crisis in 1967 he replaced James Callaghan as Chancellor of the Exchequer. As Chancellor, he maintained a tight fiscal policy to control inflation and introduced a particularly tough budget in 1968 which saw major tax rises. Labour unexpectedly lost the 1970 Election but Jenkins was elected as Deputy leader of the Labour Party in the same year. He was strongly opposed to Labour Party policy of being against entry to the European communities. Following the 1974 Election Wilson appointed Jenkins as Home Secretary for the second time. Wilson resigned 2 years later and although Jenkins stood in the Leadership Election, he finished 3rd behind James Callaghan. He resigned from Parliament and accepted the appointment as the first ever British President of the European Commission.

He regularly wrote books and in his, 'A Life at the Centre' he said his broad position was 'firmly libertarian'. He was an uncompromising internationalist and distrusted the deification of the enterprise culture and emphasised the limitations of the market. After completing his term at the Commission in 1971 he announced a surprise return to British politics and opposing Labours turn to the left under the leadership of Michael Foot, he became one of the 'Gang of 4' senior Labour figures who broke away from the party and founded the SDP. Jenkins won a by- election to return to Parliament as MP for Glasgow Hillhead, a famous result when he took the seat away from the Conservatives.

He became leader of the SDP in the 1983 Election, during which he formed an electoral alliance with the Liberal Party. After a disappointing election result, he resigned as leader and subsequently lost his seat in Parliament in the 1987 election and accepted a Life Peerage to sit in the House of Lords as a Liberal Democrat. He was elected to succeed Harold MacMillan as Chancellor at the University of Oxford and held that position for 16 years. In the late 1990s he served as a close advisor to Prime Minister Tony Blair and chaired a major commission on electoral reform. He was also a noted historian, biographer and writer.

In his personal life he was rather estranged from his working-class roots in Wales but retained a relatively happy marriage. He died at the age of 83 in 2003.

CONCLUSION

By Glyn Mathias (former political editor of ITN and of BBC Wales, and Member of the Electoral Commision).

Rarely can one say that the action of a politician has directly affected one's family, but that is true in the case of David Lloyd George. In September 1914, he prevailed in an argument with Kitchener, the Secretary for War, as to whether Nonconformists should be permitted to serve as army chaplains alongside their Anglican counterparts. It was one of many battles Lloyd George had fought on behalf of non-conformity, and it meant that my grandfather was among the first Nonconformist chaplains to serve in the army.

I was reminded of this as I travelled on Jonathan Morgan's rollercoaster ride through Welsh politicians from different ages, and I was reminded of others I had met. Here is S.O. Davies, in his eighties, striding through the streets of Merthyr in his black suit and black Homburg hat, who, when deselected by the Labour party, had the temerity to stand against them and win. Here is Tristan Garel-Jones who as a youthful Conservative candidate contested the parliamentary election at Caernarfon in February 1974. I had to film him, megaphone in hand, addressing a hillside of sheep about the dangers of a Labour government. Here is Cledwyn Hughes, a man I liked and admired, explaining to the Home Secretary, Willie Whitelaw, what might happen if Gwynfor Evans' hunger strike for a Welsh language channel came to a calamitous end. And Neil Kinnock of course, who I vividly recall singing Welsh hymns on a train from Moscow to Leningrad.

The point he is making in this slim volume is that we should recognise the achievements at Westminster of politicians from Wales, like Roy Jenkins from Abersychan, Michael Heseltine from Swansea and Michael Howard from Llanelli. That is before the era of

140

devolution when Ron Davies so narrowly won the referendum in 1997 and then steered the legislation through parliament. And Rhodri Morgan of course, who came to embody the spirit of Welsh devolution as Robin Lewis so ably describes.

He and the other guest writers provide elegant essays which provide the backbone to this book.

Bibliography

Turning the Tide: The Life of Lady Rhondda by Angela V John, Parthian Books 2014

Ann Clwyd, Rebel with a Cause by Ann Clwyd, Biteback Books 2017

A Life of Michael Foot by Kenneth O Morgan, Harper Collins 2008

Enoch Powell a Biography by Robert Shepherd, Hutchinson 1996

Rhodri Morgan, A Political Life in Wales & Westminster, University of Wales Press 2017

Geoffrey Howe, Conflict of Loyalty, Pan 1995

James Callaghan, Time and Chance, Harper Collins 1987

Roy Jenkins by John Campbell, Vintage 2015

David Lloyd George: The Great Outsider, by Roy Hattersley, Vintage 2015

Political Chameleon, In Search of George Thomas, by Martin Shipton, Welsh Academic Press 2017

Michael Heseltine by Michael Crick, Hamish Hamilton 1997

A Life of Dr Thomatoms Jones by E L Ellis, University of Wales Press 1992

Lightning Source UK Ltd.
Milton Keynes UK
UKHW021812220922
409257UK00006B/77

9 780992 869007